# Alcohol

THE INFORMED PARENT

# Alcohol

## What's a Parent to Believe?

Stephen G. Biddulph

Hazelden
Center City, Minnesota 55012-0176

1-800-328-0094
1-651-213-4590 (Fax)
www.hazelden.org

Library of Congress Cataloging-in-Publication Data
Biddulph, Stephen G., 1945-
    Alcohol : what's a parent to believe? / Stephen G. Biddulph.
        p. cm. — (The informed parent)
    Includes bibliographical references and index.
    ISBN 1-59285-040-5 (softcover)
    1. Teenagers—Alcohol use. 2. Parent and teenager. 3. Alcoholism—Prevention. 4.
Alcoholism—Treatment. I. Title. II. Series.

HV5135.B5 2003
362.292'0835—dc21
                                                                    2003050914

**Editor's note**
Any stories or case studies that may be used in this material are composites of many
individuals. Names and details have been changed to protect identities.
    "An Ancient Tale" on pages 96–97 is reprinted with permission of J. B. Ritchie.

07 06 05 04 03    6 5 4 3 2 1

Cover design by David Spohn
Interior design by David Spohn
Typesetting by Tursso Companies

# Contents

**Acknowledgments vii**


**Introduction 1**

**Chapter 1:**  Perspectives on Alcohol: From Parents, Teens, and Society **5**

**Chapter 2:**  Alcohol and the Body: What Happens When We Take a Drink? **21**

**Chapter 3:**  Adolescence and Alcohol: What's the Attraction? **43**

**Chapter 4:**  Alcohol Addiction: Is There Such a Thing as Responsible Teenage Drinking? **77**

**Chapter 5:**  A Model of Adolescent Addiction: What Happens When Kids Cross the Line? **99**

**Chapter 6:**  Reasons to Save: Can We Really Make a Difference? **127**

**Chapter 7:**  Prevention and Diversion: Can Alcoholism Be Prevented? **135**

**Chapter 8:**  Intervention: How Parents Can Help Teens **155**

**Chapter 9:**  Treatment: The Next Step **167**

**Chapter 10:**  Recovery: Regaining a Healthy Lifestyle **195**


**Notes 223**
**Index 229**
**About the Author 235**

# Acknowledgments

In writing this guidebook for parents, I stand upon the shoulders of countless others who have brought to light the knowledge and ideas upon which this work draws. Although my name appears on the cover, this was not an individual effort. I am indebted to those who have enlightened my understanding and beliefs to make this book possible. Janice Gabe, George Ross, countless researchers who wrote informative articles about alcoholism and health, the National Institute of Alcohol Abuse and Addictions (NIAAA), and Bonner Ritchie, a personal friend and mentor whose story "An Ancient Tale" has inspired me for years, are among those I wish to acknowledge.

This book was made possible by Hazelden Publishing and Educational Services in Center City, Minnesota. I am not an employee of Hazelden; however, I have been associated with the organization for several years through writing and presenting training and lectures on adolescent and family addictions. In every circumstance, I have been pleased by Hazelden's graciousness and superb commitment to excellence in providing honest and helpful materials for people in recovery. I have been the benefactor of the professionalism of the staff, beginning with Richard Solly, the editor who collaborated with me on *The Adolescent Recovery Plan and Continuing Care: A Team Approach.*

I am indebted to those at Hazelden for their support and confidence in me and for making possible the publication of this parent guide. Karen Chernyaev has been my editor and guide throughout the process of conceptualizing, formatting, and writing. Her thoroughness and personal insights have been an inspiration to me and have both broadened and personalized the message of this book. I am deeply grateful to her and to Kristin Buzick for their editorial assistance.

I wish to acknowledge Dr. Garold Barton, Ph.D., director of Clinical Services at Provo Canyon School, who has been a friend and mentor for many years, and all of my former colleagues there for making possible the experiences and opportunities that have ultimately gone into the writing of this book and others.

My wife, Elaine, has always been supportive and encouraging in this work. But most fundamentally, her true example of womanhood and motherhood in bearing and raising our six children—often when I was absent because of duties with the U.S. Marine Corps—has been the richest blessing in my life. Without her, purpose would not exist. Our children are our greatest assets and the foundation of our joy.

# Introduction

This book is a factual and informative guide for parents on the subject of alcohol use by children, especially teenagers. Each parent comes with a unique experience and perspective on the topic of alcohol, but one thing unites parents: the quandary that results when parents combine the phenomenon of teenage drinking with their own attitudes, beliefs, and behaviors around drinking. How you stand on the subject ultimately determines the role you will play in your children's lives pertaining to their use of alcohol. This book is designed to help remove the perplexity by providing parents with helpful information.

Nowhere in this book will I tell you not to use alcohol. I leave that to you to decide. Rather, it is my intention to present only facts about alcohol, alcohol abuse, and alcoholism, as known today through scientific research and practical medicine, and to provide related information to provoke intelligent thought and informed decisions. Nevertheless, I must be forthright. I would not want the reader to think that I am ambivalent on the subject of underage drinking. I do not condone it for any reason. However, it is for you to make up your own mind about alcohol and what role it will play in your life and the lives of your children.

I believe that we need to come to three important conclusions by the time we are done: (1) What role will we allow alcohol to play in our own personal lives? (2) What influence will we allow alcohol to have in our children's lives? (3) What are we willing to do about it? I invite you to open your mind to what this book has to teach.

I approach the writing of this parent guidebook from specific perspectives that I'd like readers to understand. First, I write as the father of six children and twelve grandchildren. I know teens and I understand the challenges of parenthood. My experience may not be exactly like yours, but parents have a common mission: to help children make the most of whatever their circumstances. In this regard, we can learn from each other and receive support.

Second, I write from the perspective of an adolescent therapist and addictions counselor with several years' experience. I know about troubled teens and struggling families. I know about most of the challenges that teens face growing up in this world and the dangers that entrap many of them. I know the power and influence that alcohol abuse and addiction can have in the lives of parents, children, and families. I've cheered with them when they've overcome. I've wept with them when they let circumstances defeat them.

Third, I write this book as a one-time university administrator—a dean of students—with the awesome task of administering student life. I've watched students from various backgrounds and walks of life try to integrate themselves into a demanding social and intellectual arena, many of them away from home for the first time. I've seen alcohol used as a way of having fun, of feeling good, and of gaining sexual favors. I've seen it used as a rite of passage into fraternities, sororities, and other social groups. I've seen it used in an attempt to cope with the stresses of academic performance.

As a dean of students, I served on the Virginia State Coalition for alcohol abuse. I've seen the problems faced by administrators to cope with the loss of productivity, student performance, and even lives through alcohol and other drug abuse. I've seen colleges and universities spend literally millions of dollars each year to try to curb the significant problems that surround college-age drinking and to convince students that they can have fun without drinking. I am aware of the pain of notifying parents of a student's failure or even death because of accident, injury, or misbehavior related to alcohol or other drug use.

I also write this book from a perspective of an officer in the United States Marine Corps who had numerous opportunities to lead young, vigorous, hard-charging people. The military culture of my day included drinking. Officer and enlisted clubs were the popular hangouts where Marines gathered after work for "happy hour." Weekends and evenings were spent in bars and pubs, and social events were unthinkable without a large supply of alcoholic beverages. It was a time of double standards, when many a good Marine was disgraced and punished before military tribunals because he could not hold his liquor, or was held in questionable review because he could not manage his family, finances, or job because of alcohol problems.

Last, and perhaps most significant, I write this book from the perspective of one who has a strong spiritual basis in his life. I doubt seriously that I could have survived parenthood, combat duty as a Marine in Vietnam, and the other responsibilities I have had without a personal conviction that there was something higher and more powerful than myself helping me. This conviction has brought me perspective and vision in times that otherwise would have been black holes. It has provided purpose when things seemed to have no rhyme or reason. It has brought hope and courage when I felt none. It has brought peace amid tumult. It has lifted me to be equal to tasks to which I felt unequal. It has given me longer vision and resolve in trying moments. It has given me a greater love and appreciation for my fellow sojourners in this life, a deeper respect, and a kinder heart.

Through it all, I've learned that I can never adequately judge another human soul. I can only seek to understand another's experience in life and to share mine. I've learned that I cannot save others from what I perceive are mistakes in judgment and behavior, but I can help empower them, through sharing mutual respect and lessons learned, to catch a higher, longer vision and rise above their self-imposed limitations. I believe in the creative genius of youth and parents. This book is written in that spirit.

This book is presented in ten chapters. Chapter 1 puts alcohol in perspective from different points of view. Chapter 2 provides unbiased, factual information about alcohol as a psychoactive drug and about its effects upon the human body and mind. Chapter 3 will help you understand why some kids experiment, why some don't use, and what puts some kids at high risk for serious abuse and addiction. A discussion of alcohol and addiction is incomplete without understanding why teens think and feel and act the way they do. If we hope to understand the disease, we must also understand the victim. Chapter 4 helps parents understand the cause, the symptoms, and the consequences of alcohol abuse and alcoholism. Chapter 5 provides a working model of teenage addiction to help you understand how alcohol addiction actually works in the life of a teen. Chapter 6 offers hope, providing compelling reasons to persevere with your child in spite of what may seem unconquerable odds. Chapter 7 discusses prevention and diversion strategies for those parents whose teen either has not yet begun to drink or is just becoming infatuated with it. Chapter 8 discusses intervention, treatment, and recovery strategies for those with children who are dependent on alcohol or another drug. Chapter 9 offers guidelines for choosing appropriate and effective treatment. Chapter 10 discusses the importance of a healthy lifestyle to sustain recovery and the promise of a better future.

It is my sincere desire that this book will be a source of inspiration and assistance to you as you grapple with the challenges of parenthood.

# Chapter 1

# Perspectives on Alcohol: From Parents, Teens, and Society

$W$e all have our perspectives on life—including the topic of alcohol—and they are all somewhat different because our experience in life is different. But our experience alone is inadequate on matters that have the power to affect the happiness and quality of our lives and those of our children. It is to our advantage to challenge and broaden our perspective with truth, because even our most cherished beliefs will sometimes be self-serving and misguided.

To begin the discussion of perspectives on alcohol, I'd like to reflect for a moment on our views and beliefs about alcohol. If we open ourselves to learning correct principles and expanding our understanding on these important matters, we can avoid the big potholes in the road of life. As author, educator, and administrator Neil A. Maxwell wrote, "Knowing the truth about those things that really matter frees us from our inhibiting and finite perspective in the same way that turning the light on in an otherwise darkened room can keep us from stubbing toes and breaking furniture."

Three definitions of alcohol use are important to distinguish. Not everyone who uses abuses; not everyone who abuses is addicted. People who drink alcohol fall into different categories of use and see their use differently. The terms will be treated in greater detail in chapter 5, but I will state them simply here.

5

*Use of alcohol* is the temperate, prudent, and controlled use of an alcoholic substance in a manner that does not exceed legal or health limits and that does not place the user at risk for serious physical, social, emotional, or psychological problems.

*Abuse of alcohol* is the use of alcohol in an unhealthy and risky manner, use that is excessive, illegal, or dangerous and that actually or potentially places a person at risk for physical, social, emotional, or psychological problems, such as driving under the influence or placing oneself in a harmful situation or engaging in unprotected sex.

*Alcoholism or alcohol dependence/addiction* is the loss of control of one's use of alcohol by reason, time, amount, or frequency; the obsessing and craving for alcohol; the need to drink alcohol to feel normal or functional; and a manifestation of serious and ongoing social, emotional, physical, and psychological problems related to drinking—whether the person recognizes it or not.

### A Parent's Perspective

Parents want their children to have happiness, productivity, and success in their lives. I haven't met any responsible parents who didn't genuinely want better things for their children than they had for themselves and who weren't willing to help their children achieve them. We differ occasionally on what those things are and on how they can be obtained, but for the most part, we want our kids to be happy.

About the time our child is approaching adolescence, we begin to worry about the choices our child will be faced with in middle school and high school. Adolescence is often the time when many kids are introduced to and will decide whether to experiment with chemicals. Alcohol, an accessible and socially sanctioned drug, is one of those chemicals. At some point, our child will have to decide whether to use or abstain. It's that prevalent.

Many of us struggle to know how to prepare our children for this challenge or how to address it when it begins to show itself in their lives. We don't know exactly what to say to our children about the subject of alcohol. We may not know much about it. We may feel that we do more harm or awaken curiosity unnecessarily by saying something. We may fear that if we raise the subject, our teen will be more inclined toward using out of a natural resistance to or rebellion against authority. We may feel that we will further alienate our kids or harm an already fragile relationship by "harping" on alcohol and associated behavior. Adolescence is a time when our relationship with our children is perhaps the most strained, and we may tend to shrink from any topic that might only worsen the problems. We may feel hypocritical by talking about it if we ourselves use or abuse alcohol.

No matter what our apprehension is about talking with our children, it is important that we talk to them in an honest, open, factual, and respectful manner. If we wait until we are forced into action because of alcohol abuse and consequential behavior, then a talk will be even more difficult because of increased guilt, remorse, embarrassment, or bitterness. When this parental duty of talking with our children is neglected for whatever reason, we and our children lose more than we gain.

### What Do We Believe?

*What do I believe about alcohol? Where do I personally stand with alcohol use in my own life?* What we as parents believe about alcohol and what our personal stance is on alcohol in our own lives will measurably influence how we feel about our children's use. Perhaps we already have a belief system established about alcohol or may be reevaluating it. Perhaps we use alcohol and see no harm in our child's using it. Perhaps we see our child's use of alcohol as a rite of passage into adulthood or think that occasional intemperance is a normal stage of youth that will pass along with the acne and cracking voices. Perhaps we are abstinent ourselves and have strong feelings against its use, and our child is questioning or challenging our beliefs. Perhaps we abuse alcohol or are addicted and fear that our child will do the same. Perhaps we have used in our own youth and had little or no problems, or have overcome problems, and feel that experimenting and overcoming the consequences of our actions is just an unavoidable part of growing up. Alcoholism may run in our family; it may be a problem for our parent, grandparent, or spouse. We may be unaware that we abuse or are addicted to alcohol. Perhaps our child is addicted and has lost control of his use of alcohol, and we don't know what to do about it. Perhaps we are in recovery and question how we can help. Perhaps we feel clueless about what to say to our teen or how to say it. Perhaps we are simply looking for factual information that we can use to help our children avoid problems with alcohol and other drug abuse.

Whatever our "perhaps," our experience, point of view, and influence as a parent or significant adult play an important part in our child's choices. Regardless of where we stand or what we believe, we need to be aware that children benefit from open and honest communication with us about alcohol and other drugs. If we ignore this subject, hoping that it will go away or not become a problem, rest assured, someone, someplace, sometime will teach our child about alcohol, and we may not like the outcome. Our adolescent either has already made or soon will make a decision about her relationship to alcohol. This decision will be one of the important choices she makes in her young life. Beneath all the hype and posturing, our child deeply wants and needs our counsel and guidance; she just may not know it.

## Parents as Role Models
The role alcohol plays in our own lives may influence the role it plays in our children's lives. We need to look closely at the facts and realities

of alcohol, as they are presented here and in other resources, before fully making up our mind about alcohol use. A healthy attitude on alcohol is based upon a healthy respect for the drug, upon the potential trade-offs, and upon an individual's capacity to control its use. Respect requires accurate information and good judgment, independent from our own habits and biases.

We are role models for our child, and what is safe for us may not be safe for our child. If we come to the conclusion that alcohol use is not appropriate for our teen, but we ourselves use, then we need to draw a conclusion as to why that is so. Why is it all right for us to use, but not our teen? He may see it as a double standard, and we need to decide whether the double standard is appropriate. Are we placing our child at risk by our attitude about alcohol? Are we placing ourselves at risk? If we have experienced negative consequences from drinking alcohol, then we probably won't want our child to go through what we have, but how do we communicate that without being hypocritical? If we are resolutely opposed to any alcohol use by anyone in the family, how are we going to handle it? Are we going to use scared-straight tactics or stringent controls? Are we going to ignore it and just hope that it never happens? Are we going to try to control the amount of alcohol our teen consumes? These and other scenarios are challenging for parents. We will attempt to address some of these in this book.

One of the most powerful lessons we can give to our children about alcohol, or any other topic, is by our own example. Sometimes parents think that they've paid their dues as children and that they do not need to change or grow anymore; they are now free to do what they please; it's their turn to be in charge. May I suggest that change is not just a youth thing, but a life thing. We are "becoming" throughout our lives, even as parents and grandparents. As soon as we stop, we stagnate and begin to die. Growing and improving along with our children brings legitimacy, closeness, and trust to our relationship. Children want to grow up to be better than their parents. What do we, as parents, want to become? What are we moving toward? Do we know?

Teenagers already know, from ample evidence, that we are not perfect. Their once naive belief that Mom and Dad were perfection personified has long since shattered. They will neither appreciate nor benefit from strong-armed control and power plays of hypocrisy. What they need to know is that we recognize that none of us is perfect and that, in spite of our children's imperfections, we love them just the same and believe in them. Teens need to know that we are still learning and making improvements right along with them. Heaven forbid if teens were asked to see their parents and other adults as the immutable image of ultimate human perfection. We are not! And we do our children a disservice when we refuse to make needed changes in our lives but require change of them.

Children will follow parents who lead by example, which includes parents who recognize and make worthwhile changes in their lives. Successful parents take the time and make the effort to lead from the front, not in perfection but in wisdom, humility, and personal example. Successful parents seek knowledge and wisdom beyond themselves and communicate their feelings to their children. Children need to know that their parents can be afraid or uncertain at times, and they need to see their parents address challenges in productive ways, even when things don't go as planned. They learn from this modeled behavior and are less inclined to be shoved from the rear.

### A Historical Perspective

Consumption of alcohol is almost as old as humanity. As far back as antiquity, poems and sonnets and tales have been built around the virtues and woes of this intoxicating drink. Wine was used in ancient Egypt and the use of narcotics can be dated to 4000 B.C. Wine and spirits were also used by the Greeks, the Romans, and the early Europeans for social and emotional purposes. In antiquity, wine, made from the fermentation of grapes, was the almost exclusive alcoholic drink. Later, other variations were discovered, such as forms of ale and rum. In many cases, wine and other forms of alcohol were considered safer to drink than the water that was available.

It appears likely that the ancients did not understand the scientific process of brewing and that wine was more the result of naturally occurring fermentation. However, it's clear that wine—even 2,500 years ago, as evidenced to by the Greek lyric poet Alcaeus—had intoxicating potency and was believed to be useful for relieving stress. Even the Bible makes reference to individuals becoming intoxicated with wine. But not until the nineteenth century did people learn how to extract the active ingredients of alcohol from malt and hops through fermentation and brewing to mass-produce alcohol with varying percentages of strength. Thus, alcohol became more powerful and its use more widespread for pleasurable purposes.

In the 1800s, alcohol, as well as other psychoactive drugs, began to be prescribed and used throughout Europe, the United States, and other parts of the world without any controls. Tinkers, alchemists, showmen, drugstores, and traveling salesmen freely advertised alcohol as a cure-all for ailments, both physical and emotional. Saloons and clubs and other establishments came into existence as centers of mostly male sociability built around alcohol.

In time, excessive alcohol consumption became a real social problem. Alcohol became a scourge of society, especially in England and the United States. Men particularly were prone to drunkenness, which led to abusive and rude behavior, broken homes and marriages, and other social ills. Women, tired of the negative effects of alcohol on their families and communities, began organizing and speaking out in an effort to either abolish or at least curtail alcohol use. It is interesting to note that temperance movements existed even in ancient times, indicating a long history of problems with alcohol abuse. In 1919, the U.S. Congress passed the Eighteenth Amendment, prohibiting the manufacture, sale, and consumption of alcoholic beverages.

In response to this prohibition, the era of private stills and illegal bootlegging began. Many people were determined to have their liquor one way or the other. Prohibition lasted until 1933, when the Eighteenth Amendment was repealed through the strong influence of special interest groups because it was seen as too restrictive to human rights and because it hadn't successfully stopped the problems anyway. People decided that legalization combined with education and limitations was the better way.

The temperance movement gave rise to a close study of alcohol to provide some objectivity to alcohol's reputation as "the Devil's brew," a moral decadent, and a destroyer of human life. As a result, much study has been done on alcohol and its relation to the human mind, body, and spirit. The research has been instrumental in helping us gain a clearer, more honest perspective on alcohol.

It is generally held, on the basis of this research, that alcohol does present dangers and can become troublesome, especially for kids. It has the potential to become addictive. It has been the cause, or a partial cause, of accidents, injuries, disease, deaths, crime, and domestic violence. We understand this dangerous reality, especially for our underage children, and we have passed laws in all fifty states that ban drinking alcohol under age twenty-one and driving under its influence, and states have established legal limits for drivers' blood alcohol content (most at .10 percent, many at .08 percent).

Yet alcohol remains desirable to many people. Alcohol has been at the heart of social, leisure, and recreational activity for people around the world for at least two centuries. It is difficult to think of a man-made product that is more deeply and persistently ingrained in our psychosocial lives than alcohol. It is legal, affordable, convenient, accessible, and for the most part socially acceptable.

Alcohol is the most widely used drug in the United States, according to a recent National Longitudinal Alcohol Epidemiological Survey. An estimated 177 million Americans (81 percent) have tried alcohol at least once in their lives. Nearly 113 million Americans over the age of twelve (52 percent) currently drink alcohol.[1]

Alcohol is legally promoted in the media. Its advertisements are among the cleverest and most attractive on television. Companies that sell alcohol are major sponsors of popular social and sporting events and alcohol is widely publicized in movies. It is enmeshed in some religious and cultural populations. Alcohol is so common and accepted in our society that most people don't think of it as a drug like other abused drugs, such as barbiturates, cocaine, heroin, or methamphetamine.

Statistics show some decrease in alcohol use during the 1990s. Information compiled by the U.S. Department of Agriculture shows that both per capita alcohol consumption and production of alcoholic beverages decreased noticeably between 1986 and 1999. Alcohol-related traffic fatalities declined 29 percent. Drinking and driving arrests were down overall. Alcohol-related violent crime rates declined along with the decline in the use of alcohol. Yet alcohol use among teenagers remained fairly stable over the past several years, averaging 24 percent for eighth graders, 40 percent for tenth graders, and 51 percent for twelfth graders. Also, binge drinking (consuming five or more drinks in a row) by the same age groups remained consistent at 15 percent, 26 percent, and 31 percent, respectively. In other words, alcohol use among teens remains a significant national social problem.[2]

**A Look into the Future**
State and federal governments have recognized the continuing concern with youth drinking. So pervasive is this problem that states

have begun to form coalitions with academic, civic, and spiritual organizations to promote awareness and to create drug-free environments for youth. Governments are placing greater emphasis on proactive methods of prevention and diversion, rather than on reactive treatment. For example, greater emphasis and support is provided to families, school, and other community institutions to educate youth and families on the dangers of alcohol use: DARE (Drug Abuse Resistance Education) programs are an outgrowth of such work. Communities and schools provide healthier diversionary activities and programs to keep youth involved and to care for latchkey children. Advertisements emphasize parents talking with youth about drugs and youth talking to youth about "just saying no."

Considerable effort is going into research on alcohol problems—on causes, consequences, treatment, and prevention. Scientists believe that human genes may hold the secret to addiction. Science has known for a considerable time that addictive traits are passed genetically from parent to child, just like other physical characteristics: hair, eyes, features, and so on. Through powerful microscopic techniques, scientists are seeking to identify and measure the role of genes in heavy drinking. As a result of this research, scientists may be able to help prevent and treat alcoholism with medication.

Studies of the brain have already led to the development of anti-craving medications called naltrexone and acamprosate. While not appropriate treatment for everyone, these medications work best with behavioral therapy.

Treatment modalities have been developed to help people addicted to alcohol and other drugs recover their sobriety. Researchers have studied several of these traditional methods, including motivational, cognitive-behavioral, and Twelve Step programs, to determine which are the most effective. Interestingly, they have discovered that all of the above methods are helpful when coupled with total abstinence from drinking and are useful in leading people to a lifetime of recovery. We have discovered that in addition to sustained abstinence, people must overcome destructive and self-defeating beliefs, thoughts, feelings, behaviors, and relationships that contribute to their abuse of alcohol. We have learned that sustained addiction in children significantly impairs important developmental tasks, leaving them physically, emotionally, and socially stunted.

## A Teen's Perspective

A teen is a product of many things: age, physical development, social influence, family values, and learned behaviors. The natural transition from childhood into adulthood is characterized by amazing physical, psychological, and emotional changes raging within. No other time in human life (after the age of two) is as impactful and filled with change as is adolescence.

Depending upon our teen's childhood experiences, she may look at the world with hope, enthusiasm, and self-confidence, or she may regard it with fear, uncertainty, and doubt. She may enter adolescence with a well-developed repertoire of skills or relatively few. Whatever the situation, our teen does not see the world from our adult eyes—wise and perhaps somewhat jaded by the realities of living—but from the young, eager, impulsive eyes of one hungry for adult privileges and status.

Our teen is in discovery, both of himself and of the adult world around him, and he discovers that life is challenging and complex. He is becoming a new creature with a new, adult body, the capacities of which usually exceed his emotional maturity and wisdom to govern effectively. He is curious, temperamental, impulsive, emotional, and very much in need of acceptance. In fact, the less certain our child is of his own capacities and inherent worth, the more he seeks confirmation and acceptance from friends, peers, and associates outside the family.

A teen explodes into her environment, stretching against family values and rules, questioning, challenging, reaching beyond the relative safety of home. She is driven to go places, do things, and be with friends. All of this is new and sometimes unsettling to parents. Teens lacking self-esteem, self-confidence, a strong bond with parents and family, and a set of internalized values are at high risk for succumbing to negative influences, including alcohol and other drugs.

As parents, we should know how our teen views alcohol or how much of an influence it may have in her life. It should not surprise us that alcohol is the number one drug of choice among American teens, surpassing tobacco and other illicit drugs. An estimated 60 percent of people ages eighteen to twenty-five use alcohol. Nearly 14 percent of these are heavy alcohol users. An estimated 33 million Americans (15.6 percent) who drink, including 38 percent of people eighteen to twenty-five years of age, reported binge drinking.[3]

Alcohol is not difficult for kids to get. Seventy-one percent of eighth graders and 88 percent of tenth graders believe that alcohol is readily available to them for consumption.[4] Teens who find easy access to alcohol from adults tend to use. Of schoolchildren who reported drinking, 46 percent said that they obtained it from a person aged twenty-one or older.[5]

Kids experiment with alcohol more than any other drug, including tobacco, and at young ages. For instance, statistics released in 2001 indicate that 41 percent of ninth-grade students reported having consumed alcohol before they were age thirteen, as compared with 26.2 percent reporting smoking cigarettes and 11.6 percent smoking marijuana. Girls used to drink considerably less than teenage boys but that gap has closed markedly over recent years. Among ninth graders, girls consume alcohol and binge drink at rates almost equal to boys.[6]

Children of today are exposed to alcohol early in their lives by parents, relatives, and other friends and by media advertising.

Unfortunately, some encountered it as a fetus and bear the physical and psychological disabilities of fetal alcohol syndrome (FAS) and other cognitive disabilities. Alcohol is legally marketed to children directly into their homes as a highly desirable but forbidden adult pleasure through attractive, youthful television ads and other media. Recent advertising expenditures in the United States for beer, wine, and liquor combined totaled $1.4 billion, twenty times the amount spent on milk ads. Alcohol is a regular part of leisure activities, and alcohol companies sponsor local and national events enjoyed by families. From the time children are old enough to understand, messages are sent to them that alcohol use is accepted, expected, and even essential to having a good time.[7]

Teens are tuned in to and influenced by what's going on around them because they are continually judging themselves according to others and the values that the world tells them are important. Teens with little solid grounding are highly susceptible to social stimuli. Modeling behavior is important to teens, especially that of people they admire or want to be like. Beer commercials and other influences suggest that if you are "with it" and "cool," you must be in the party scene; to be adult, you must drink. Adolescents are looking for fun and entertainment today, not responsibility or peace or long-term benefits. They live in a here-and-now world. The more aware of beer commercials a teen is, the more favorable his belief about drinking seems to be and the more apt he is to express an intention to drink frequently.[8]

A large number of teens have personal experiences with the effects of alcoholism in their lives. Approximately one out of every four children is exposed to addiction or abuse in the family before the age of eighteen.[9] This exposure is often frightening or discouraging and can place them in dangerous, even life-threatening, situations. A serious family addiction—especially in a parent—can stunt a child's social, emotional, and psychological development. Sometimes this experience leads a teen into her own abuse because of emotional trauma, and sometimes it acts as a strong inhibitor, the teen not wanting to experience the same problems she's seen in adults.

Most teens are influenced by their peers, especially close friends. Peer use of alcohol is a strong predictor of alcohol abuse by teens. When our child's peers and friends use alcohol, the chances of his using are increased significantly. Continued pleading and pressure applied by peers can break down even the strongest of kids if left unchecked and unsupported by family and other social systems. If we doubt the pressure our child may be under, consider that 30 percent of fourth through sixth graders reported that they received "a lot" of pressure from classmates and peers to drink beer.[10] It is both naive and unwise of us to think that somehow our adolescent is exempt from this type of pressure.

Families are important factors in teen use of alcohol. Research shows that children drink less and are less likely to have drinking problems when parents are involved with them on a regular basis, they feel they have a close relationship with their parents, and parents provide limitations, clear expectations, and discipline.[11]

This is true because our children—even impulsive teenagers—still, deep down, want and value the love and respect and protection afforded them by their parents and family. This is almost universally true. Most children know that their parents love them. They do not have to earn that love. But they do have to prove themselves in the world outside the family. That is one reason that they place so much importance on outside relationships. However, they still need and crave the love and acceptance of their family, even though they may have suffered disappointment and pain because of family members and even though they may occasionally—even frequently—violate family values and rules.

## Double Messages

The flaunting of the forbidden fruit before our children has worked so effectively that by the time they are fourteen years old, over half of them have tried alcohol at least once, and one in four is using regularly (weekly or even several times a week). By age sixteen, those who have tried alcohol at least once jumps to seven out of ten, and four of them are using regularly. By age eighteen, eight of those ten children have tried alcohol, and half are using regularly. During the teenage years, a child's chance of abusing alcohol increases by nearly 50 percent.

The use of alcohol by children and adolescents is not the moderate social use of many mature adults. Kids use alcohol to get drunk. Of eighth graders who reported the use of alcohol, 25 percent reported being drunk in the previous thirty days. That figure climbs to 30 percent by tenth grade and 50 percent by twelfth grade. Binge drinking by adolescents also increases with age: eighth grade, 15 percent; ninth grade, 25 percent; tenth grade, 26 percent; and twelfth grade, 31 percent.[12]

Nearly 14 million Americans (1 in every 13 adults) grow up to abuse or become addicted to alcohol, and millions more engage in out-of-control risky behavior that can lead to alcohol problems.[13] It's possible that our attempts to curtail underage use of alcohol have been hurt by our double message: it's okay for us to use but not for you.

## Youthful Deception

Many teens who are under treatment for alcoholism state that alcohol was deceptive to them in the beginning because it was such an accepted and available drug. They felt almost compelled or pushed into drinking in some cases. Their parents used or it was heavily advertised as a desirable drink. Adults around them even winked at and tolerated their use of alcohol as teenagers. It seemed so innocuous, so desirable, so adult, and they didn't see the harm until they lost control of their drinking and it became a problem. Suddenly, they found that all the tolerance and winking disappeared and turned into turmoil, disgust, punishment, and negative consequences. Suddenly, drinking wasn't okay.

# Chapter 2

# Alcohol and the Body:
# What Happens When We Take a Drink?

**N**ot all kids who try alcohol or even get drunk will go on to be alcoholics; only a minority do. Many will abuse, perhaps even through college, and then lose interest as responsibilities and other priorities take over in their lives. However, two crucial concerns arise with underage drinking: the short-term danger and the longer-term unknown factor of potential addiction. When a teen consumes alcohol, he generally doesn't use it wisely. That is, he won't limit himself to one social drink. More often than not, drinking is taken to some level of drunkenness. This places him in a potentially dangerous and compromising circumstance for accident, injury, disease, misbehavior, and even death. It also numbs the teen's natural feelings and interferes with important developmental tasks. Sometimes drinking can bring a teen into conflict with social norms and laws that can hinder his progress, harm his self-esteem and reputation with others, and limit his potential for success in school, athletics, and other areas of personal achievement. A teen also does not know whether he is a potential alcoholic until it is too late—by trial and error. Once discovered, the road back to sobriety can be difficult and steep.

### The Drug We Call Alcohol
The primary ingredients for all addictive substances are part of our

natural world. For example, alcohol is made up of three essential elements in our world: oxygen, carbon, and hydrogen. Some substances are naturally occurring and others are created by chemical processes. When chemically combined, substances can be altered into toxic products. Alcohol is produced through fermentation and brewing. Through this process, oxygen, carbon, and hydrogen become *ethanol*, or *ethyl alcohol*, which is used widely in medicine, science, industry, and alcoholic beverages. The chemical composition of alcohol is the same in all alcoholic beverages; some beverages, however, have more alcohol in them than others.

Each of these compounds that we call drugs or chemicals has different properties. Because each human body is uniquely different in its physical makeup, different chemicals can have varying effects on different individuals. For instance, cold medication—which often contains alcohol—has no effect upon me other than to help relieve the aches and pains of a cold. If my wife, on the other hand, takes the same medication, she can't sleep, her mind races, and she is generally overstimulated. Some chemicals have special psychoactive properties that others don't have. When abused regularly or heavily, psychoactive substances can irreparably change, even destroy, a human life. Alcohol is among these substances.

## What Is a Psychoactive Drug?

The term *psychoactive* is given to certain drugs that have the power to affect human psychology. The brain controls a person's psychology; that is, the way she thinks, feels, and behaves, including moods, desires, and physical coordination. A drug is any chemical or chemical compound used as a medicine to treat physical or psychological ailments or that is used for social or recreational purposes to get high. A psychoactive drug is one that has the power to penetrate the central nervous system (CNS) and affect cognitive, emotional, and behavioral functions. When used in medicine, psychoactive drugs regulate or ameliorate maladaptive behavior or psychological disorders. Because of their properties, psychoactive drugs are also drugs of abuse.

Psychoactive drugs may be classified into four broad groups: (1) stimulants, (2) hallucinogens, (3) inhalants, and (4) depressants. Each affects the CNS in a different way.

## Stimulant

A CNS stimulant is a drug that speeds up (stimulates) parts of the central nervous system and, in turn, the body. The slang term for stimulants is "uppers." Stimulants fire up the body's nervous system by releasing significant amounts of chemicals (neurotransmitters) and artificially stimulating the body with large amounts of energy and sensations of pleasure. Stimulants produce feelings of overconfidence, pleasure, invincibility, and power. Some common stimulants are cocaine, amphetamines, methamphetamine, diet pills, caffeine, and nicotine. Stimulants are dangerous in that they can overstimulate the body's systems, causing seizures, strokes, heart attacks, and emotional paranoia; damaging vital organs; and provoking dangerous behavior.

## Hallucinogens

Hallucinogens are also called psychedelic drugs, or "all-arounders," because they are known to produce wild and contorted hallucinations in the mind and can take on the effects of either a stimulant or a depressant, depending upon the chemical makeup of the user. Common hallucinogens include LSD, mushrooms, DMT, peyote, STP, marijuana, and PCP. Hallucinogens generally distort the sensory system of the CNS, causing visual and auditory hallucinations. Hallucinogens can cause dangerous emotional, cognitive, and behavioral acting out. Teens are harmed or killed by hallucinogens mainly because of the make-believe world of illusions the drug creates, often resulting in dangerous and irrational behaviors. Use of these drugs harms vital organs, including the brain's capacities to think, remember, and reason. Even onetime use has been known to kill or irreparably damage developing brain cells. Powerful hallucinogens can permanently affect the sensory system and cause persistent hallucinations known as *flashbacks*. Pot is not normally thought of as a psychedelic because it does not generally induce the pronounced hallucinations of more powerful drugs, such as LSD or PCP. Nevertheless, it is included in this same family of drugs because it carries the same qualities in smaller, less obvious forms.

## Inhalants

Inhalants are chemical vapors breathed in through the nose and mouth, a process called "huffing." Inhalants are cheap, easily available, and harmful. Common inhalants used by kids include nitrous oxide, amyl nitrite, butyl nitrite, and chlorohydrocarbons found in aerosols, paints, cleaning fluids, solvents, gasoline, glue, and paint thinner. Inhalants are taken directly into the lungs and blood stream and reach the brain quickly and with great power. Inhalants destroy brain cells and damage other vital organs. They can kill a teen by causing heart arrhythmia, strokes, blackouts, and seizures. They also cause violent, out-of-control behavior and can damage the CNS permanently.

Inhalants are attractive to teens and unattractive to adults for the same reasons: they are common, unsophisticated, accessible, inexpensive, and offer a quick and powerful high. Kids don't usually have a lot of money to spend on drugs and their drug use habits are often rather unsophisticated. Teens often don't understand the significant dangers of huffing inhalants that adults do, or they simply don't care or don't believe that inhalants can hurt them. Those who are looking for a quick, cheap high find it in huffing.

Depressants

A CNS depressant is a psychoactive drug that depresses or slows down the CNS and numbs the brain by releasing chemicals that shut off pain and other discomfort centers and release additional chemicals that enhance the pleasure centers of the brain. The slang term for depressants is "downers." Common depressants include opium, codeine, morphine, heroin, and *alcohol*. Depressants are physically addicting and can irreparably damage vital organs if taken for long periods. They are dangerous if taken in too large a dose because they shut down body functions, such as respiration, circulation, and other essential processes, and prevent the user from properly caring for herself. Excessive abuse of alcohol causes irreparable damage to important cells of the body, resulting in loss of or diminished intellectual functions, such as memory and thinking. Heroin and barbiturates are known to be much more powerful—potentially lethal—and more addicting than alcohol, but unlike heroin, alcohol is known to cause damage to every vital organ in the body.

I'll say more later about alcohol as a CNS depressant. Suffice it to say for now that alcohol is classified as a CNS depressant because it depresses or slows down body functions, such as heart rate and breathing, and also disrupts the ability to react to stimuli in a timely manner.

**What Is the Central Nervous System?**

The central nervous system is composed of the brain and the spinal cord. It controls everything that happens, consciously and unconsciously, in the body. It can be likened to the master electrical panel in a home, composed of switches that turn on and off the electrical power to various rooms and appliances that make our home useful, comfortable, and pleasant. One switch runs the heating and cooling, others the stove, refrigerator, lights. The power comes into our home from an outside source to this master panel and runs through the switches, which can be turned off automatically or manually. If the outside source delivers too large a surge of electricity, more than the system can handle, the switch automatically kicks off to protect our home or appliances from burning up. We can also manually turn off the power to our house by flipping the switch on the panel.

Similarly, our bodies have a built-in electrical and chemical system to regulate it. The sympathetic nervous system, one part of the CNS, speeds up body functions, causing breathing and blood flow to work faster or harder when we exercise or are frightened. The parasympathetic system, in contrast, causes body functions to slow down. Thus, the body is able to regulate itself and keep balance.

The CNS of the brain exercises control through miles of nerves (which we can liken to the electrical wiring in our home) that act as communication channels that regulate the functioning of organs and muscles (our body's appliances and functions). The CNS receives sensory messages from all parts of the body and sends messages that help regulate how we perceive, process, think, feel, act, and react in life. This communication is done with chemical and electrical impulses. Tiny bits of chemicals (called neurotransmitters) link nerves together and transmit messages along the passageways. When people introduce psychoactive drugs—including alcohol—into their CNS, it artificially changes the system by increasing or decreasing the flow of neurotransmitters. Thus, the brain can become sluggish, confused, or overstimulated, or can shut down. Drugs can generate hallucinations; change moods, thoughts, and behaviors; and retard physical performance. When used heavily or for extended periods or, in the case of very powerful drugs, when used even once or just a few times, they can alter permanently or for extended periods of time the remarkable sensory system of the body, causing dependence and changing the life of a child.

Alcohol, as a CNS depressant, plays a role in affecting virtually all of the body's systems, including the respiratory, circulatory, digestive, endocrine, reproductive, muscle, and skeletal systems. While alcohol is not known to have some of the dramatic, short-term effects on the CNS that some other drugs have, it can cause dysfunction sufficient to produce injury, poor judgment, accidents, and social problems. Over the long term, alcohol abuse can cause disease and death and permanent disability in people. More important to teens, alcohol abuse can disrupt the normal development of the body's vital systems during adolescence, which can have lifelong effects. Alcohol abuse has a more profound and lasting effect on adolescents than it does on mature adults, who have completed their growth cycles.

**The Body's Chemical Balance**
As mentioned above, the systems of the human body that sustain a healthy, productive life are governed by chemicals called neurotransmitters. The human body comes preprogrammed with a finely tuned balance of these chemicals. Sometimes it isn't perfect, but it's quite remarkable. These chemicals regulate most of our bodily functions, acting as important transmitters of stimuli and response. For example, some chemicals send messages of pleasure or satisfaction; some of fear, sorrow, alertness, activity, pain, humor, or tiredness; and some send sensations of temperature. Others regulate growth and development. Our body is constantly sensing its environment and sending messages to the brain and receiving reactions.

The central nervous system contains billions of nerve cells, each with tiny neurotransmitters that communicate important messages throughout the body. Psychoactive drugs are capable of penetrating these chemical areas. When administered by trained physicians, the right drugs can help balance deficiencies. When abused, a psychoactive drug, such as alcohol, cocaine, or heroin, can disrupt and confuse the body's systems and its interpretation and reaction to stimuli, sometimes permanently and fatally.

## Pathways to the Brain

The human body is designed to take in food and other things in almost all forms: gas, vapors, liquids, solids, creams, and lotions. It is equipped to swallow, to inhale, to absorb, or to be injected, but no matter how psychoactive substances enter the body, they find their way into the bloodstream and pass through major organs, including the brain.

Some passageways reach the brain faster and with stronger effect than others. For example, injected or inhaled substances reach the brain faster than something taken orally or by absorption through the skin. Liquids and solids taken in through the mouth are digested in the stomach and the intestines and transferred into the blood for distribution throughout the body. Gases and vapors inhaled through the nose and mouth go into the trachea and lungs and are absorbed into the bloodstream. Creams, lotions, and oils are absorbed through the pores of the skin and into the bloodstream. Liquids may also be injected with needles directly into a vein.

Alcohol is taken into the body mainly through the mouth (orally) because of its liquid nature, although people have been known to inject alcohol directly into the bloodstream with IV needles to avoid the smell of alcohol on the breath. A binge drinker may insert a flexible plastic tube down the throat directly into the stomach. Large amounts of alcohol are poured through a funnel in the tube directly into the stomach, allowing for the ingestion of large amounts of alcohol in a very short time. This is called "beer bonging." Beer bonging can cause acute alcohol toxicity (poisoning) and death because of the rapid and high rates of alcohol taken into the bloodstream. Beer bonging causes the death of hundreds of college-aged students each year.

## How Does Alcohol Affect the CNS?

Many people don't think of alcohol as being in the same class as other depressants that are abused because it doesn't appear to be as dangerous or potent when taken into the body. Usually, a drink or two of alcohol doesn't send a person into a wild and spacey high as some drugs can do. When a person drinks too much, often the worst he experiences is a hangover, not a life-threatening overdose. Drinking frequently does not manifest the obvious and immediate deleterious effects that heroin or cocaine or LSD does.

The truth is that alcohol works on the brain in ways similar to nicotine, heroin, or marijuana. One of the ways alcohol affects the brain is through a chemical transmitter known as *serotonin*. Serotonin directly influences how fast and efficiently the brain is able to send, receive, and store information from the body. The amount of serotonin in our brain affects our ability to learn, remember, and perceive and respond to our environment. It also affects our moods. Researchers have shown that alcohol increases the release of serotonin, flooding the nervous system and interrupting our ability to learn, as well as to control our body, our mind, and our emotions, much like a heavy surge of electricity through electrical wires will blow a circuit. The nerve endings within the nervous system become clogged or altered and unable to effectively transmit information.

Serotonin actually influences many bodily functions, and researchers believe that an increase of serotonin through alcohol use may contribute to physical dependence on alcohol, a condition called alcoholism. Alcohol is also known to increase a chemical called gaba, which serves as an inhibitor in our brain. This increase in gaba impairs our ability to think rationally, to remember things, to use good judgment, and to coordinate our body muscles.

Another chemical messenger associated with the CNS is *dopamine*, which regulates the body's reinforcement of pleasure, satisfaction, and motivation. When we engage in something pleasurable, dopamine is released, infusing the CNS with a sense of satisfaction, thus reinforcing the act that brought about the pleasure and motivating us to repeat the process. Research has shown that even low doses of alcohol can increase dopamine release in the nervous system, producing pleasure and reinforcing alcohol consumption. Heroin does the same thing.

One might rightfully ask, "What can be so bad about feeling good?" It's not the feeling but the way the feeling is gained and the aftereffects that can be harmful. Actually, alcohol is artificially forcing our body to release high levels of dopamine into the nervous system,

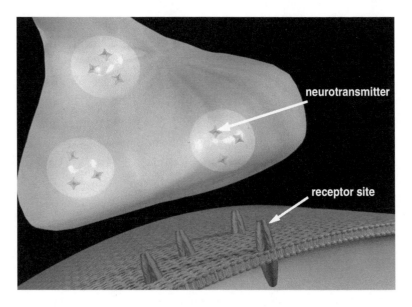

The brain is programmed to release enough neurotransmitters to fill the corresponding receptor sites of the next cell. Drugs, including alcohol, mimic neurotransmitters and fill receptor sites, telling the brain to stop producing neurotransmitters. When the drug is gone, the natural supply of neurotransmitters is depleted. (Adapted from NIDA images)

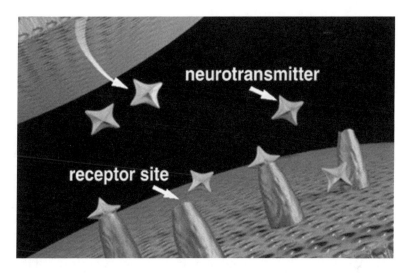

making us feel pleasure and numbing our sense of reality. The body has only a certain amount of dopamine and is capable of regenerating only so much in a given time. Thus, if we use it all up through the use of alcohol, we can bankrupt our dopamine account, leaving us impoverished in our ability to experience normal pleasure.

Studies on the use of methamphetamine have shown that these powerful drugs can destroy, sometimes permanently, the body's ability to generate pleasure from normal activities and experiences in life, leaving the abuser unable to find pleasure or happiness in the simple things and dependent on the artificial stimulation of dopamine by drug use. Alcohol does not normally wield the same power as methamphetamine, but its effect upon the pleasure pathway is essentially the same, and if abused for varying amounts of time, alcohol can cause dependence, or addiction. Over time—sometimes quickly, depending upon the chemical makeup of the individual—the tiny receptors in each nerve where dopamine is produced, released, and received are changed, so that pleasure is no longer generated through normal stimuli but requires the presence of alcohol. Eventually, not even the presence of alcohol can provide pleasure. Thus, an affected person may not find pleasure in a family outing, a good dinner, a fun movie, or an athletic event but requires getting drunk or at least consuming sufficient amounts of alcohol to create an artificial feeling of pleasure. When the temporary fix wears off, an alcoholic is overcome with a drop or crash, which fills him with physical, psychological, and emotional pain, or at least strong discomfort.

If taken in excess, psychoactive depressants can shut down the CNS, causing blackouts, seizures, and even death. We can stop breathing. We can stop receiving important stimuli from the environment, or the stimuli becomes distorted and confused, or we become unable to respond appropriately to stimuli, often resulting in life-threatening accidents and injury. In other words, too many of the important switches in the master control panel get turned off, making us vulnerable to injury or death. Thousands of people actually die every year from alcohol-related accidents and violence, and many others die from an overdose of alcohol because the alcohol shuts down the CNS. Teens are particularly vulnerable.

**How Does Alcohol Abuse Affect My Teen?**
Many adults use alcohol moderately and prudently without any significant problems. "Moderate," "careful," and "prudent" do not normally describe adolescent drinking. Many parents used alcohol as teens and came out just fine, and many still use alcohol in responsible and controlled ways. The truth is, a majority of teens follow the same course. However, it is the significant exceptions to that rule—the kids who die, are seriously injured, contract serious diseases, or have their lives forever changed by addiction—that should concern us, and it is the uncertainty about which camp our teens will fall into that should make us diligent.

Teens, by nature, tend to think that they are untouchable, invincible, and immune to accident, injury, death, and health problems, and their beliefs about alcohol follow the same line of thinking. Especially today, life seems fraught with dangers and risks. It may be immeasurably more dangerous to walk out of our home every day and go to school or drive a car than to have a drink of alcohol. Indeed, it is difficult to believe that a product that is marketed and endorsed and used by so many can be potentially dangerous. A teen might easily justify use of alcohol by saying, "It's fun, it makes me feel good, it's adult, and it won't hurt me." So we want to be careful that we are responsible in our views about alcohol. If we as parents understand the powerful potential effects of alcohol on adolescents, we are in a better position to help our children see beyond the here-and-now mentality and have a better chance at avoiding potential problems with alcohol.

## Risks

An extensive body of information has been compiled over the years about the risks and benefits of alcohol. Not all of it is accurate or useful, nor is it absolute or universal in applicability. The truth is, we can twist information to justify whatever we choose to believe. Perhaps we are wiser to adjust our beliefs to fit the knowledge of what is true. Each of us must decide for ourselves what is true and whether we will follow the truth. For this reason, I've included information about the risks of alcohol use among teenagers. Because alcohol is legal for adults, accepted, accessible, available, and affordable, it is the drug most widely used by teens. The information that follows on the risks of teen alcohol use is based on some of the most recent and reliable laboratory research and on statistics from human demographics.

### Memory Loss

Adolescents who abuse alcohol may remember 10 percent less of what they have learned in a given period of time than those who don't drink.[1] Loss of memory is one of the noticeable complaints of teens who have abused alcohol and other drugs, such as marijuana, amphetamines, hallucinogens, and inhalants.

## Psychological Distress

Among twelve- to seventeen-year-old drinkers, 31 percent had extreme levels of psychological distress, and 39 percent exhibited serious behavioral problems.[2] Girls twelve to sixteen who drink alcohol are four times more likely to suffer depression than nondrinkers.[3] This is interesting in the light of many who view alcohol as a stress reducer. Of course, we cannot say which came first, stress or drinking, but it is apparent that whenever teens are doing something illegal or that brings them into conflict with family, religious, or social norms, stress results. Teens who use alcohol to have fun or feel good or who drink to fit in or on a dare are more likely to drink to excess, and their actions tend to be more thoughtless, spontaneous, and attention-getting. This type of behavior, more often than not, results in consequences that increase stress.

## Teen Suicides

Of reported suicides by children ages nine to fifteen, 28 percent have been attributed to alcohol.[4] One in every four children who take their lives does so under the influence of alcohol or because of alcohol-related circumstances. Alcoholic teens may be more prone to take their lives, especially if they are feeling depressed and hopeless. Some children who live in alcoholic homes and are subjected to emotional or physical abuse or neglect can also become suicidal, especially if they have no other support system or outlets.

## Diseases and Health Risks

Adolescents who drink heavily assume the same long-term health risks as adults who drink heavily. It is difficult for a teen or parent to see into the future. We tend to worry more about the present danger of accident or injury due to drinking. Yet drinking can lead to alcoholism, and prolonged alcohol abuse will ultimately lead to an erosion of health. The speed with which that happens is dependent upon the individual and cannot be categorically stated.

Youth ages twelve to sixteen who drink alcohol have higher blood pressure than nondrinkers.[5] High blood pressure can lead to health problems, most notably strokes and aneurysms caused by the rupture of blood vessels in the brain. There is no evidence to suggest that alcohol-induced strokes are prevalent among teens, although there have been such cases.

Adolescent females who drink exhibit higher levels of the hormones *estradiol* and *testosterone* in their bodies. Estradiol is a form of estrogen that has been linked to diseases such as breast cancer in older women. Research seems to show a correlation between increased quantities of estradiol and increased risk for breast cancer at some point.[6] High levels of testosterone are also common in people with increased risk for substance abuse.[7]

Alcohol is frequently tied to sexually transmitted diseases, including human immunodeficiency virus (HIV), and to unwanted pregnancy. This is because alcohol is often a catalyst for loss of social inhibition among teens who are partying together or socially interacting. Teens are coming of age in a world that condones and promotes premarital and extramarital sex and doesn't view abstinence or self-control as options. Intoxication places a young man or woman at increased risk for sexual contact because of reduced judgment and self-control. Young women who are intoxicated become easy targets for men with sexual appetites. The AIDS virus is most noticeably spread through sexual contact, and condoms are proving ineffective as a protection, with up to 50 percent failure rates in some instances.

The hepatitis C virus (HCV) is an inflammation of the liver and can result in liver cancer and cirrhosis or scarring of the liver. It is a major cause of death in the United States. Alcohol has been clinically shown to increase the risk of acquiring the hepatitis C virus and to make the virus worse once contracted, even in people who do not show classic risk factors, such as intravenous drug abuse or blood transfusions. Alcohol promotes inflammation and fibrosis in the liver, both harbingers of rapid and severe progression of liver disease. Additionally, alcohol has been shown to impair the body's immune defense against the virus, thus making a person more susceptible to contracting HCV and less able to overcome or throw off the virus once contracted. The antiviral treatment given to patients with HCV produces some side effects, and alcohol is known to exacerbate these side effects.[8]

Research has shown a relationship between HIV infection and heavy alcohol use. Many people who are at high risk for HIV/AIDS are also heavy drinkers. By interfering with the central nervous system and impairing the immune system, alcohol increases susceptibility to HIV infection. Perhaps more important, chronic alcohol abuse is thought to increase the adverse effects of HIV and may be a contributor to HIV resulting in acquired immunodeficiency syndrome (AIDS).[9]

Alcohol consumption has been linked to an increased risk for various cancers, most notably mouth, esophagus, larynx, stomach, colon, rectum, liver, breast, and ovarian.[10] There is no conclusive evidence that alcohol, by itself, causes cancer, but it does promote or speed up the effects of other cancer-causing agents, such as tobacco. In other words, when alcohol and tobacco are consumed together, alcohol can enhance the possibility of contracting cancer from tobacco. In fact, over 75 percent of cancers of the upper digestive and respiratory tract are attributed to a combination of alcohol and tobacco.[11]

Drinking during pregnancy, even moderate social drinking, is shown to increase the risk of fetal alcohol syndrome (FAS) and other learning and behavioral problems as the child grows.[12] These are devastating tragedies that damage the unborn child's CNS, resulting in irreversible physical and mental defects that are harmful to the quality of life of both child and parents.

Adolescence is a time when bone is maturing and gaining strength. Alcohol has been shown to reduce peak bone development in the immature (adolescent) skeleton, resulting in easier fractures and increased problems with bone loss (osteoporosis) in later life.[13]

### Injury and Mortality

Alcohol is implicated in more than 100,000 deaths annually, compared with only 16,000 for all other drugs except tobacco (430,000). One person is injured every two minutes in an alcohol-related accident in the United States.[14] When alcohol consumption goes down, so do traffic accidents and deaths and criminal violence.

### Poor School Performance

Teenage alcoholism and school failure are linked. While many people who have used or even abused alcohol as teens have gone on to become successful adults, many do not and often struggle mightily in school and other areas of their lives. Alcohol use can sabotage a student's ability to consistently meet the rigors of schoolwork because it clouds mental capacities and influences motivation and attitudes about school achievement. A survey of eighteen- to twenty-four-year-olds who failed to complete high school showed that nearly 60 percent of them began drinking before age sixteen.[15]

### Delay in Puberty

Research indicates that even moderate amounts of alcohol on a regular basis can suppress the excretion of sexual hormones, thereby disrupting or delaying the normal timing and progression of puberty in adolescents.[16] Abnormal development of puberty can cause a child significant distress, resulting in the failure to develop self-esteem and self-confidence, which, in turn, affects attitudes and behaviors. I've known teens who were teased mercilessly by peers because of slow development to fail in school, get into negative behaviors and drug abuse, and even commit suicide. I've also known teens who were prematurely introduced into drinking, partying, and sexual relationships because of their early physical development (facial hair, breasts, and other characteristics).

### Male Reproductive System Problems
Alcohol use lowers testosterone levels and other reproductive hormones in males. These hormones are important to normal body functions, including growth, development, metabolism, and reproduction.[17]

### Legal Offenses and Violence
Two million (38 percent) of the nation's convicted offenders—adults and teenagers—were drinking at the time of offense by their own report. Heavier drinking increases the potential for problems at home, work, and in society, including arguments, separations or divorce, strained co-worker relations, absenteeism, tardiness, loss of employment, crimes, and violence. Alcohol use is also shown to promote fights, assaults, quarrels, and other violence at school and after school.[18]

About one half of the sexual assault offenses committed by adults in the United States involve alcohol consumption by the perpetrator, the victim, or both. Alcohol use places teens in risky circumstances and relationships. It eliminates normal defenses, diminishes good judgment, and induces behaviors that are regretted later. Teenage rape, date rape, assaults, and pregnancies are associated with alcohol use.[19]

## Driving

Studies over the years have shown that a driver under the influence of alcohol has impaired vision, perception, judgment, and reaction because of alcohol's inherent effect upon the central nervous system. Alcohol slows the process of transmission of stimuli from the senses to the brain and back to the muscles, slowing down reaction times and diminishing coordination, both crucial to driving, especially on busy highways. Each state has a legal limit for blood alcohol level, usually at .10 or .08 percent. Studies show, however, that alcohol diminishes driving skills at levels lower than those established as legal.

Among drivers aged fifteen to twenty, fatal crashes involving a single vehicle at night are three times more likely when alcohol is involved.[20] These statistics come from emergency and police enforcement reports. Drinking is known to impair reactions, attentiveness, and judgment.

Of all children under age fifteen killed in vehicle accidents in 2000, 20 percent of them were in alcohol-related crashes.[21] "Alcohol-related" means that the people involved in the accident were using or under the influence of alcohol at the time of the crash, as reported by survivors or as determined by occupants' blood alcohol content.

## Medications

More than 150 medications, including antidepressant, cold, and allergy medications, pose potential dangers when mixed with alcohol. When alcohol and other drugs are mixed or taken simultaneously (polysubstance abuse), they can potentially react with each other to create powerful and sometimes potentially lethal overdoses.

## Binge Drinking

At one-third of the colleges surveyed, more than half of the students classified themselves as binge drinkers. Binge drinking was most prevalent among students in fraternities and sororities, at 81.1 percent. Approximately two of every five American college students can be termed binge drinkers.[22]

## Benefits

Research indicates that small quantities of alcohol may increase estrogen levels in women who are postmenopausal, thus reducing bone loss and helping to prevent osteoporosis. This is less apparent in women who are of reproductive age.[23]

A moderate amount of alcohol (moderate is defined as one eight-ounce drink per day for women and no more than two eight-ounce drinks per day for men) may also help prevent heart attacks and strokes in adults.[24]

There is some suggestion that moderate alcohol use can reduce stress, but as already indicated, that has not been conclusively proved, and alcohol's stress-reducing benefit varies according to a person's physical state, gender, genetic makeup, current social and emotional stress levels, drinking circumstances, body weight, and other factors.[25]

When many adults prudently use alcohol in moderate amounts, they find alcohol provides social and leisure enjoyment.

The risk statistics presented in this section are not meant to scare but to inform. It is inappropriate to imply that any drinking of alcohol will result in serious problems. While there are some benefits for adults, as indicated above, they do not apply to teens or to adults who are chemically dependent. The risks heavily outweigh the benefits.

The facts I've listed are just a sampling of what scientists are learning every day about alcohol. Any other product with as many defects and potential harm as those of alcohol would be banned by the U.S. Food and Drug Administration and immediately removed from store shelves. People would, in fact, be suing manufacturers for damages. Yet, for some reason, we seem to make exceptions for alcohol.

# Chapter 3

# Adolescence and Alcohol: What's the Attraction?

**A**ny discussion of alcohol abuse and alcoholism is incomplete and almost meaningless without discussing the potential victims: the teens. This section looks at the nature of teens as developing adults and the reasons why some teens are at higher risk for alcohol abuse and addiction.

### New Beginnings

Adolescence is a period of powerful transition and change. It is a time of awakening, of new beginnings, of transition, and of unparalleled growth. In fact, no period of time in human development, save the first two years of life, can compare to adolescence when it comes to development and change.

Out of the generally benign and protected world of childhood emerges the teenager, faced with the daunting task of becoming an adult in an increasingly demanding world. Our teen is learning who he is, what he values, and what he can become. His body is evolving into a full adult, with all the powers and appetites and feelings that accompany adulthood. He is discovering similarities in and differences between what he is taught in his family and in larger society.

A teenager is learning how others in this big world will accept and respond to her. She is deciding if she can compete in this world and what makes her unique or special. She is in the process of making the transition from a self-absorbed state of "me" to becoming part of something bigger, but it is still very much about her. She feels that everybody is watching her and judging what she does. Healthy growth is a process of transition from self-absorption and self-justification to becoming more other-focused.

Newly equipped with physical and sexual powers and presented with new and exciting opportunities and interests, teens lack the maturity of years, the wisdom of experience, and the fully developed capacity to reason with logic. It is an exciting yet challenging time for a teen. He may be fearful or uncertain about himself. He may be running as fast as he can toward adulthood with unbridled gusto and excitement. He may be running away from the pains and discomforts of childhood. He may be caught in difficult transitions by psychological, physical, and mental challenges that make competing in the adult world difficult and discouraging.

Our child's perception of his potential in the world of adulthood is determined by what he has learned from his role models and what he has experienced thus far in his life. We who were once perfect and superhuman in our child's eyes have become flawed and out of touch with reality. Our teen may begin to question rules, policies, and family traditions as unrealistic, unfair, or undesirable. He begins to look beyond us and other family members for role models and support. It is not that he necessarily wants to reject and abandon his home support system, but he wants to free himself from home base and explore the intriguing and exciting world beyond.

Adolescence is characterized by moodiness and emotional volatility. Not only are the hormones in flux, but teens also have intense concerns about acceptance by others and about competitiveness. Teens are seeking to achieve emotional independence from their parents. They can be grumpy, noncommunicative, sarcastic, and sullen. I remember as a teen going through entire meals without saying a thing, and when someone spoke to me, they were greeted with a grunt. Yet when my mother caught me at the front door on my way to high school and said, "You're going to be a great man someday," I walked to school a little taller and with more confidence. Of course, I never told her that! Moods and behaviors can sometimes be so volatile and so uncharacteristic of the children we knew that it can seem that they are no longer our children.

Alcohol abuse and alcoholism affect our teen's already volatile moods and behaviors. The mood of alcoholic teens can change—rather quickly—to sullenness, volatility, anxiety, and depression. Their lifestyle often changes: choice of music may evolve toward drug-related lyrics; they may give up old friends for using friends; they can become negligent and defiant about chores and expected roles; their sleeping and eating patterns can change; their behavioral changes might include staying out late, sleeping late, extreme tiredness, loss of appetite, unwillingness to participate in family activities, truancy from school, or conflicts with school and community officials.

Of course, some of this type of behavior is also typical of normal adolescent changes, so it can be difficult for parents to tell the difference. However, there are ways to tell whether the changes are due to hormones or alcohol use. We should look at our entire teen, not just at one symptom, such as a change in moods. We can look at friends and relationships, school performance, family, emotions, and work ethic, and make comparisons and draw inferences. Alcohol abuse becomes more visible when we look at the many dimensions of a child's life.

### Products of a System

Teens are products of the system in which they are raised. By system, I mean all of the forces at work in a child's life that create and shape his beliefs, attitudes, and values. This system influences him physically, psychologically, developmentally, spiritually, socially, and culturally. The system provides opportunities that can both help and hinder his development. The system begins in infancy in the home and continues through adolescence in the larger society.

In referring to this system, a coalition of governors' spouses made the following observation about children and alcohol:

> Children draw conclusions about alcohol-related social norms from what they see and hear about alcohol in their families and communities. These norms strongly influence their own attitudes and behaviors regarding alcohol. When communities consistently prevent underage access to alcohol, publicize and enforce alcohol-related laws, and limit the promotion of alcohol, they reinforce the message that alcohol use by young people is unacceptable.[1]

Each child and each system is different. However, there are some broad generalities that apply to all.

### The Physical Component

Our child's body is perhaps the most significant influence in her life at the age of adolescence. So much of her self-esteem and self-identity is tied up with her body image. The importance of the physical diminishes with time, but during adolescence it's a big deal. It's interesting how little direct influence she has over her body. She's pretty much stuck with what she gets. She can make some cosmetic changes, but for the most part, she is what she inherits. Her body comes with a pre-programmed genetic blueprint that determines much of her physical attributes and capacities. She is discovering, becoming, evolving within that blueprint, and her self-esteem and self-confidence can be influenced by how she turns out. She makes comparisons with her friends and peers and with the "ideal" images that society projects.

Some of our greatest challenges as parents can lie in helping a child accept physical reality and understand that it's not what nature does to him that matters but what he does with what he gets. A recent documentary on overweight children struck me as interesting. Many of these children were genetically predisposed to heaviness and found themselves discriminated against and on the fringes of peer acceptance. Others were obese because of the junk- and fast-food lifestyles and little exercise. One young girl—perhaps fourteen—had obviously been coached by her parents and perhaps other caring adults to grasp the reality of her obesity and to make the most of it. She was watching her diet, curtailing many foods desirable to youth, and becoming involved in a physical weight control and exercise program. Further, she was excelling in developing her talents in music and service to others. She had caught the vision of her internal worth and was making the best of her situation. I know of many teens who are so distraught by their physical appearance that they just give up and become self-destructive, often by using drugs and alcohol.

Here are some questions to consider:

- What physical challenges make our teen's life abnormally distressful?
- How is he handling it?
- How are we as parents helping our child do the best he can?
- Does our family have a history of alcohol problems or addiction?

### The Development Component

Most teens emerge from the developmental phase of adolescence fairly unscathed and intact, but they may face some challenges that can cause distress and vulnerability. The timing with which our teen achieves puberty and other significant milestones can influence self-esteem and behavior. A teen's physical body will become adult before her mind and emotions become adult. Social, emotional, and reasoning capacities almost always lag behind physical development. So, for example, she is rather suddenly beset upon with strong emotions and urges related to the opposite sex that she hasn't learned to emotionally cope with or control. She may have the physical capacity to "make love" through sexual activity, but she lacks the emotional-rational capacity to understand mature love. She can create babies, but she isn't prepared to parent one, nor should she be. She may feel that she is a woman now with her new adult body and that she wants to have the privileges and opportunities available to an adult. But she is not emotionally and psychologically prepared to control it.

A child who develops early or late in adolescence can have self-esteem challenges. A teen who physically develops earlier than his peers often finds himself under new and challenging pressure to act like an adult, when emotionally he is not prepared to. For example, a boy who develops facial hair or other noticeable mature traits earlier than his peers is often idolized by others and is easily accepted into an older age group, with increased expectations to perform and with new challenges that he may not be prepared to handle. A well-developed girl suddenly finds herself the attraction of older boys and is invited to parties that may not be safe or healthy for her. In contrast, teens who develop late can have trouble fitting into their peer group. Sometimes they are made fun of or criticized as being weirdos, causing some distress and leaving them vulnerable to potentially negative repercussions.

There are other stresses. Some teens suffer with psychological problems and serious physical and emotional trauma that leave them hurt, scarred, and distrusting. Children who have little self-esteem or who don't trust anyone, who are short on social and communication skills, or who have other problems that inhibit fitting in with their peers are at high risk for problem behavior that could involve drinking and other drug abuse.

- Has our child experienced any abnormal development for extended periods of time? Has it caused noticeable distress?
- How has our teen been treated by family, peers, and others?
- What roadblocks to successful living has our child experienced?

### The Psychological Component

Even mentally healthy teens have volatile emotions and impulsive behavior. It is just part of the hormonal process as teens learn to look at life through different eyes and with new feelings. Usually, these emotions are worked through in adolescence and the teen emerges as a stable adult. However, if strong emotions are not properly limited, disciplined, or resolved, they can place a teen at risk for social conflicts and dangerous misbehaviors. Teens need to learn not only how to cope with strong emotions but also how to resolve negative ones so they do not get in the way of their happiness and success. Often, this just takes someone who cares enough to listen to them and guide them, someone in addition to Mom and Dad. It takes someone whom they can respect and who can bring out the best in them, someone like a coach or teacher.

Some children also experience disabling psychological disorders that interfere with successful behavior. These include problems with mood, affect, adjustment, anxiety, cognition and learning, personality, and behavior. Many very bright children have learning disabilities. They are not "dumb" but are limited in their ability to concentrate, focus, and assimilate or retrieve information, or they have problems grasping reading and math. Anything that prevents children from feeling normal or successfully fulfilling their own and other's expectations causes great distress and can result in hopelessness if not resolved. Discouraged children are at risk for self-defeating behaviors. Some of them seek self-medication or social-emotional relief through alcohol or other drugs.

- Has our teen experienced any of these problems?
- How have we handled the problems?

### The Social Component

An important task for teens is to establish their own identity. This sense of who they are begins first with parents and home life, but then rapidly expands into the broader society with peers, friends, and other people. The search for identity is a major reason that teens are so socially minded, so friend crazy, so caught up in fads and fitting in. Most teens discover a healthy sense of identity, but some do not because of problems they may encounter during this time.

Children generally thrive in families and communities that provide healthy environments, good values, and opportunities for constructive development. Research shows that communities where alcohol abuse is tolerated or condoned and where a large number of establishments serve alcohol produce teens more likely to engage in underage drinking and to have problems later in life.

The social skills teens develop also play a role in their identity. Most teens develop a fairly good set of social skills and adjust fine, but some don't because of problems that prevent this important development. Teens stunted in social skills are often excluded from the mainstream and are labeled as different or undesirable. They may become discouraged or hopeless. They may feel that they cannot fit in with normal society, so they excel at being different. Our teens will migrate toward people and behaviors that fit their self-image and will find acceptance among peers who provide them what they are looking for. For teens it is all about acceptance.

- Does our teen have a healthy self-identity?
- What kind of neighborhood do we live in?
- What school and community extracurricular activities is our teen involved in?
- Does our teen's school have a no-tolerance policy and a strong education program on alcohol as well as other drugs of abuse?

## The Family Component

Family is where our child first experiences life and learns about herself. Personal worth and life skills are first taught here. Our child gets a sense of identity, self-esteem, and self-confidence in the home first. In the home, she learns to trust herself and others. Family will either provide for a teen's basic values and standards or it will not. If strongly imprinted on her, her values and standards will guide her in major decision making, even in adolescence. It is natural for our teen to test family values against the bigger system. Sometimes she will make impulsive decisions that are contrary to what she has been taught, but values that are positive and consistently modeled by parents and other family members are resilient strings to keep her attached in a healthy way.

We know from considerable research that children coming from family environments where alcohol is prized, where alcoholism or abuse is present, where social deviance is accepted, and where social and educational opportunities are not provided are more prone to abuse alcohol.

## The Learned Component

Much of how our child behaves and handles himself is learned behavior, or mimicking of others whom he admires or thinks is cool. Our child learns first from us, as parents and family members, and then learns new behaviors from peers, neighbors, schoolmates, and other role models. Studies show that children are more likely to behave positively when they have positive role models whom they respect and when they are supervised and coached by healthy role models. We cannot hope to provide all learned behavior within our own home; that would probably not be healthy. We should want to have our children taught and influenced by other "healthy" people, provided it doesn't compromise important family values. As parents, we can help our children learn from others without compromising values by (1) maintaining a strong bond of closeness and respect with our child; (2) maintaining a sound set of values, standards, and expectations for our child; and (3) maintaining a firm consistency in limit setting and fair discipline.

- Who are our teen's heroes?
- Do our family and support groups provide positive role models?

### The Cultural Component

In addition to the family, our child's religious, ethnic, and regional culture is a strong influence in his life. Cultural values help influence a teen's development of values and, when in harmony with those of the family, provide positive support to teens. When cultural and family values counter each other, they create conflict and stress.

Larger cultures can have microcultures buried within that attract teenagers and sometimes compete with the family for loyalty. Sometimes these microcultures are called pseudocultures. They include gangs, peer groups, and other social organizations that attract teens who need to fit in with a group. These groups can be positive or negative, depending upon their purpose and the values and behavior they promote among their members. As parents, we need to be aware of pseudocultures and of our teen's interest or participation in them.

A positive example is the Boy Scouts of America (BSA). Adolescent boys enjoy the culture provided by BSA that promotes loyalty, service, and other positive qualities. By age fourteen, boys begin to lose interest in uniforms and such, but they still enjoy hiking, camping, and high adventure. By age sixteen, they are also interested in social and occupational things, but they still need the values of scouting. All five of my sons stayed involved in BSA and earned their Eagle rank because Mom and Dad stayed involved and other role models helped out.

Addiction to or serious abuse of alcohol has its own culture. It is a powerful culture that includes its own values and standards, norms, and expectations of its members. Addiction takes priority over all other values that conflict with its demands. By itself, it is powerful, but when linked to another support group of peers, it becomes even more persuasive.

High-risk teens are those who do not succeed or thrive in normally established parts of the system. If our teen lacks positive and well-defined family and cultural values or is not thriving in her family, school, and social cultures, she is probably stressed and discouraged. She may be willing to turn to something less desirable, such as outlaw values, subcultures, and substance abuse. The abuse of alcohol can also draw a healthy teen away from a positive lifestyle and healthy values.

- What does our religious culture, if any, teach about alcohol and drug use?
- How does our ethnic culture view alcohol and drug use?
- What views does our extended family hold about alcohol and drug use?
- What influence does the culture that we currently live in provide?

The National Institute of Alcohol Abuse and Addictions (NIAAA), in its publication *Strategies to Prevent Underage Drinking*, concludes:

> Adolescent alcohol use is one of the most difficult behaviors to change because alcohol use is so ingrained in the U.S. culture. Adolescents choose to consume alcohol, not just because of personal characteristics, such as personality type or level of social skills, but also because it is a part of daily life in their communities and, for many youth, in their homes. Numerous social and environmental influences affect adolescents, including messages they receive from advertisements, community practices, adults [including parents and older siblings], and friends about alcohol.

### Why Do Kids Use Alcohol? A Look at High-Risk Teens

It is unfair and often untrue to paint a high-risk kid as a drug or alcohol abuser or a troubled kid who goes around hating and fighting and causing trouble. Many high-risk teens—even those who are addicted or involved with serious abuse of alcohol or other drugs—are sensitive, feeling people. It is equally wrong to say that a teen who is addicted to alcohol or another drug is a troublemaker, dangerous, or criminally minded. I must say that almost every teen I've counseled is—down deep—a good kid. High-risk teens are simply teens who are at higher risk than a normal teen for certain problems—in this case, alcohol abuse and addiction. High-risk teens are kids whose system has failed them or who have somehow failed to adapt in a positive way to their system.

On my desk, I keep three rocks that remind me of the high-risk kids I serve. Aha! That doesn't mean that I view them as rocks. No.

The rocks remind me of a teen's inherent worth and the high risk each one faces in life when moving through childhood and adolescence, and into adulthood. Life can be challenging, and high-risk kids face an especially difficult and dangerous task. As parents and as role models, we can help prevent, divert, and recover our children when we understand the circumstances of high risk.

## Hidden Worth

The first rock on my desk is a geode, actually half a geode. This geode is a rough, rather ugly, unattractive, dull, brown rock on the outside. But it's not the outside of the rock that I value, rather the inside. The geode has been cut in half. The inside, which has been polished until it shines and feels smooth as glass, is a surprising swirl of beautiful chocolate, red, and creams. In its center is a cavity filled with miniature, delicate crystals that sparkle and dance with light.

Geodes are like high-risk teens in a way. A teen can appear ugly or unattractive, even dull on the outside, but inside is where the real unique beauty lies, and until that beauty is realized and exposed, it remains hidden and unexpressed. The truth is, we don't know exactly how unique and beautiful each soul really is deep inside because a teen will often keep it hidden safely away and the rest of us may not take the time or effort to see deeply.

High-risk kids are those who do not recognize or realize their inherent worth. They face challenges in their lives that form a crust around their inner beauty and potential. The outer crust of the rock is made by the outside influences of nature and weather. Similarly, the outside crust of a troubled teen is formed by outside influences that cover up his beauty, worth, and potential. Being illiterate; feeling ugly; having poor social skills; or living with chronic illness, troublesome psychological problems, poverty, serious family dysfunction, neglect, or abuse can prevent the development of a beautiful nature.

Perhaps the single most absent trait noticeable in troubled teens is self-esteem. They do not perceive themselves as having worth or value, or they hide their talents. Usually, this is caused by failure to find happiness, acceptance, and success in their endeavors. They often do not trust themselves to make decisions or to find success or happiness in life. They are often followers of other dysfunctional children because they distrust "normal" people and the system as a result of rejection or past failures.

The perception of negative self-worth comes in several ways. Some of the more common are (1) inherited disabilities or disorders that prevent thriving and acceptance; this includes physical appearance that places a child at risk of social rejection or stigma; (2) accidents, injury, or other traumatic experiences that inhibit or stunt normal emotional and mental development; this includes all forms of physical, sexual, and emotional abuse, as well as neglect; (3) false beliefs, negative attitudes, and self-defeating behavior learned from and reinforced by parents, family members, or other significant people during early years and childhood; (4) lack of bonding, limit setting, and discipline in early years; (5) learned behaviors from negative role models in society; and (6) failure to develop psychological autonomy.

One of a few things can happen to such children: they kill themselves; they simply shrink away into oblivion; something happens that awakens them to their worth and they begin to thrive; they abuse drugs to equalize the emotional pain; or they remain ugly the rest of their lives. They are normally frustrated, discouraged, unhappy, even angry children and are at high risk for anything with the potential to make them feel alive, worthwhile, or powerful over their environment. Teenage alcohol abuse and the pseudoculture that often surrounds it fill that void and provide an escape from reality.

Alcoholism interferes with the cutting and polishing of the soul, leaving the beautiful luminescent colors of a teen's life secluded under ugly behavior. The crystals of light that dance and sparkle in her life are often dark and encased with discouragement and disappointment. It is possible for this inner unique beauty to disappear, for the cavity of light crystals to fill up, and for the teen to evolve into something ugly and repulsive throughout. But that usually takes time and pressure. Most troubled teens are yet geodes filled with hidden potential beauty.

Parents and responsible adults have a choice as to how they will see a teen. They can choose to see the "ugly" residue or the unusual and unique beauty. They can see reality or real potential. Those who look deeply, who are geologists of the soul, will see the beauty that others refuse to see. It is the inside of a teen that matters, not the outside.

## Hidden Pain

In the deserts of southern Utah, one can find small, round stones called desert marbles. They are made of desert sand that forms into a ball and develops a hard, metallic-like shell on the outside. The red-colored iron mineral in the desert sand combines with the oxygen in the air and water to form a hard, almost metallic substance known as iron oxide. Inside this hard shell is a ball of compressed sandstone that is still soft enough to be easily scratched out with the fingernail or a stick.

Most high-risk kids are like desert marbles. They have a soft, emotional interior and a hard exterior. Most of the teens I have worked with present a pretty hard, resistive shell. They are kids who are frequently failing at most of the important things in their lives, such as school, family relations, jobs, friendships, and self-esteem. They may have begun to have legal problems and other social conflicts. They may be stealing, involved in violence and other crimes, dangerously sexually active, and running away from home. They may be depressed and giving up on life. They may isolate themselves from others and have suicidal thoughts. A majority of these kids are at high risk for getting involved in drinking alcohol or abusing other drugs, and kids who are alcoholics or seriously abusing alcohol are at high risk for these feelings and behaviors.

The thickness of the shell around high-risk kids depends on the cause and duration of the problems in their lives. There's usually a great deal of emotional pain, including guilt, shame, grief, and self-loathing. When the cause of problems involves deep emotional trauma or long-standing psychological problems, the shell becomes much thicker and the inner emotions more rigid.

Just as the red iron mineral in the soft sand of a desert marble bleeds out and combines with oxygen and water to form a hard, protective shell, painful experiences can cause the typical teenager's need for love, acceptance, guidance, and achievement to bleed and combine with other things to form dangerous and self-destructive behaviors, appearance, and demeanor. This hard, resistant shell insulates the soft, inner emotions from positive resolution and from outside help and further deepens the pain and hopelessness.

### Hardened Life

My third example is petrified wood. Petrification happens when soft cellulose wood becomes covered with hot volcanic ash. For thousands or millions of years this wood is under pressure and heat. During this time, water, carrying various minerals, seeps down through the buried wood and replaces the soft wood molecules with hard mineral molecules from the surrounding ash. The replacement of molecules is so precise that the image of the wood is completely preserved, even down to the growth rings, bark, and wood fiber. In time, what was once soft, pliable, usable wood becomes stone that resembles wood but is useless, although sometimes beautiful.

Some high-risk kids remind me of petrified wood, especially those whose lives have been traumatic, painful, or troubled for long periods of time or who have suffered seriously debilitating problems for which no one has found satisfactory solutions. Human petrification occurs in far less time than in wood. Children begin like pieces of soft, pliable wood, unique in color, quality, and form. They can be cut and shaped and molded into all kinds of beautiful and useful people. Circumstances in life can cover them up and put them under significant pressure. Negative experiences in life can begin the process of petrifying their lives. When damaging experiences, feelings, or circumstances are prolonged without relief, teens eventually become discouraged or hopeless. Eventually they may give up, rebel, turn to drinking or drug abuse, or commit suicide. Over time, they become hardened throughout and practically unrecoverable.

**Why Do Some Kids Refrain from Drinking?**
Some kids don't use alcohol. If the statistics are correct, about 30 percent of high school seniors don't use alcohol, and an even higher percentage of younger kids are abstinent. Some of the kids in this category may try alcohol, use a few times, then quit. Why do these kids not use? Why did they choose to quit? There are at least as many reasons kids don't use alcohol as there are for using. Here are a few.

- They don't like the taste of alcohol or the way it makes them feel.
- They are repulsed by the intoxicated behaviors or the sickness and throwing up of family members, friends, and peers.
- They are determined not to repeat family patterns.
- They are involved in sports, school clubs, groups, and church groups that require certain standards of conduct to which they are committed.
- They value academic achievement and have strong life goals.

- They are attracted to a strong, sober peer group.
- They are afraid of legal problems or disappointing their parents and family members.
- They value obedience to social and family rules more than they do perceived fun or excitement with friends.
- They have internalized a moral code of conduct from their parents, families, communities, and churches.

### What Helps Promote Abstinence?

Research indicates that kids are less likely to engage in underage drinking when some or several of the following conditions exist (this is not intended to be a complete list):

1. Bonding: Children who enjoy a strong sense of bonding with parents and siblings will be more inclined to communicate with them and rely upon them for guidance and support and to discuss the topic of peer pressure and their own thoughts, questions, and concerns about alcohol use. They will be more concerned about pleasing their family because of the love that is shared.

2. Role modeling: Parents and siblings who do not drink or drink very discreetly and modestly are set up to be stronger influences and role models for their teens for abstinence.

3. Monitoring: Teens who are guided in positive structure of their time and home environment are less likely to be bored and left alone to make their own decisions. High-risk situations are more readily recognized by parents and acted upon before they become problem areas.

4. Supervision: Parents who stay actively involved with their children, showing interest in their activities and participating when possible, earn the respect and appreciation of their chil-

dren. They also understand their children better and can identify danger signals more quickly.

5. Limit setting: Parents who engage in active limit setting and
consistently fair discipline give their children a clear signal that
they are valuable and that certain things are a high priority.

6. Establishing values: Parents who transmit to their children––
in a consistently loving and respectful way—a sound set of
moral values help ground their children against a complex,
confusing, and shifting world. Teaching a child a standard of
obedience by personal example as well as precept, and by
emphasizing it, helps internalize important values.

7. Communication: Children benefit from healthy, open communication with their parents and other significant adults.
Shutdown or failure to communicate leaves children isolated
and vulnerable. Parents who listen as well as speak—and
when they speak, do so with respect and kindness, instead of
preaching and ordering—have a stronger rapport with their
children.

8. Community support: Communities and neighborhoods that
actively promote abstinence as a value and require such
behavior strengthen teens against outside influences. This is
done through laws, rules, limits, guidance, and services.

9. Activity: Positive extracurricular activities that teach communication and life skills and help teens learn important skills for
success make teens less susceptible to drinking.

10. School support: Failure in school erodes self-esteem and is one
of the biggest contributors to child delinquency. When parents, teachers, and administrators administer a program that is
child-sensitive, that helps children to be successful in school
with a strength-based approach, children have a better chance
of maintaining interest and motivation.

11. Self-esteem: Children who possess high self-esteem and good social and life skills are more likely to thrive in a social setting and are less likely to become involved in delinquent behavior and alcohol abuse. Parents, teachers, clergy, and community leaders should teach and provide opportunities for children to develop these important skills.

12. Skill development: Parents can help their children develop the ability to make healthy decisions and effectively solve problems. Such skills are taught by modeling, guiding, and coaching children. Helping children achieve a sense of psychological autonomy (confidence in their own abilities to make their own decisions with the help of others) gives them the gift of self-discipline and leadership and makes them less likely to be indiscriminate followers.

13. Work and service: Children who have been actively taught to work and to value service to others develop a self-confidence and sensitivity and work ethic that helps them throughout their lives. Children who are self-absorbed, selfish, and ungrateful are children who are lazy and want something for nothing. This type of attitude can be conducive to teenage drinking.

14. Spirituality: Parents who bequeath upon their children a strong spiritual and religious orientation and a belief system that encourages faith and hope and trust in things higher and more powerful than themselves give their children a power that is superior to any other. This faith will strengthen the spiritual resolve that controls physical appetites and helps them overcome serious challenges in their lives.

Obviously, not all of these conditions will exist in a teen's life, nor need they all be present. Our teen will have strengths and weaknesses. However, the attributes or conditions listed above, which promote a sense of self-esteem and internal values—which cause him to feel loved and respected and confident—will produce positive results in the other areas of his life. Positive teens usually do positive things.

## Why Do Non-High-Risk Kids Begin Using Alcohol?

What about the teen who is not one of these high-risk kids, who's just a normal, high-energy kid? Does that mean that she is never going to try alcohol? Or could she become a problem abuser, or even an addict? The answer to that question is that we won't know unless she drinks.

Underage drinking typically has roots in three areas of a teen's life, whether he is at high risk or not: *personal*, *social*, and *environmental*. Researchers have found that these risk areas have repeatedly been associated with alcohol use among teens. In high-risk kids, these factors are just more acute. Many of these predictors can manifest in early childhood.

### Personal Factors

#### Wanting to Feel Good

All kids are at some risk for alcohol abuse while growing up, but a majority are not what we would call high-risk kids. Most are fairly normal children just going through growing pains. Those kids who use alcohol begin using to feel good. It's that simple! They want to feel happy and crazy or that they belong to a social group that's important to them. Feeling good can also mean getting relief from stress, anxiety, or emotional pain. Even non-high-risk kids have these feelings in our increasing tumultuous and challenging world.

#### Boredom

Many teens I've worked with admit that they started using or were introduced to alcohol and other drugs because they were bored, had nothing constructive to do, nowhere productive to go, and along came an invitation to experiment with alcohol. These were kids from all walks of life, not just the kids who hung out in ghettos and slums. Boredom in a teen is an open invitation to try something that promises to be fun, exciting, and different.

### Curiosity

What teen is not curious, especially about things that are taboo or forbidden to her? Many teens haven't made up their minds about drugs or alcohol. Many kids don't know how their parents feel about the subject because their parents have never told them. In such a circumstance, a teen can easily be convinced to explore and just try it. Patterns of curious users are sporadic, unplanned, and inconsistent.

### A Desire for Fun and Excitement

Fun and excitement are what teens are usually looking for. Some don't think about the source or the consequence of the fun; they just see the lurid colors and the thrills. Alcohol and other drugs can appear this way. Patterns of preliminary use are related to enjoyment and getting a rush. If dependence sets in, the fun element is traded for the need to sustain. The fun users are typically social users who stoke the fires of exciting activity with a drink—or a drunk.

### Resentment or Rebellion

Rebellious teens are discouraged teens who have been thwarted in their efforts to succeed in positive ways and who have been hurt. Willful disobedience usually stems from feelings of anger, resentment, inadequacy, or discouragement. Angry or discouraged teens may choose to drink as a means of rebelling against parental or social rules or expectations. I've known teens who have engaged in drinking and drug use to "get back" at their parents for some real or imagined offense, who felt a need to rebel—not just question or disagree, but actually fight against their parents' authority. Alcohol use was one way for them to exert their independence and to make a statement of their hurt or resentment. Patterns of use for this symptom are typically fraught with high emotion.

*A Need to Cope with Strong Emotions*
Some children don't know how to handle their strong emotions and may turn to alcohol for some type of relief or coping mechanism. As with resentment and rebellion, anger can be a motivating force for a teens to strike out against parents or their circumstances by using alcohol. Patterns of use for this symptom are typically excessive, destructive, harmful, and combined with strong emotions.

Some teens will use alcohol to cope with stress, anxiety, or fear. Patterns of use may be sporadic or situational; that is, they will use only when they feel these strong urges or needs. Sometimes the use of a drug may help them calm down or cope more effectively during the period of use.

*Abnormal Development*
A child who has abnormally rapid or slow development, especially when he is at the stage when social life is so important, can be at risk for alcohol and other drug abuse. A child who develops prematurely may experience increased pressure and expectation to be mature and do adult things, and alcohol is an adult thing. Any experience that blocks a teen's self-esteem, self-worth, or self-confidence places an otherwise "normal" child at risk for discouragement, depression, and anger, which can result in dangerous behaviors such as drug and alcohol abuse.

*Early Childhood Behavior*
Personality characteristics such as novelty-seeking behavior, strong

exploratory curiosity, thrill-seeking, low harm avoidance, risk-taking, hyperactivity, impatience, aggressiveness, or overcompliance are indicators that may be visible to parents when children are as young as three years of age. Children with such characteristics require extra attention and structure, along with patience. Aware of such characteristics early on, parents can help children gain insights and personal skills that minimize them and subjugate them to more productive ways of behaving. When possible, parents can structure their children's environment to be as positive and productive as possible.

## Social Factors

### Peer Influence

Teens who associate with peers who drink are significantly more likely to drink themselves. Peers remain one of the stronger influences on teens to use alcohol, especially if other personal, social, and environmental factors are at play. According to a 1995 national survey of fourth through sixth graders who read the *Weekly Reader*, 30 percent said that they got "a lot" of pressure from their classmates to drink beer.[2]

### A Need for Acceptance

Teens who are excluded—for whatever reason—from one group will look elsewhere for acceptance. Many kids I've worked with found themselves on the outside of a group and so turned to a group that was more accepting. Teens who drink and use drugs are often less discriminating and selective. The only prerequisite to entrance into the group is to use and perhaps participate in the activities associated with the drug use. Use typically corresponds to social groups and involvement, which are often dangerous, illegal, or harmful. If a teen becomes addicted, the alcoholism continues independent of the social setting, and a child will use alcohol because of the craving for the effect, thus, becoming an end in itself.

### Parental or Sibling Use and Modeling

Kids who live in homes where alcohol is used are more likely to view such behavior as normal and acceptable. They sometimes even view it as the model of mature adulthood. Most often, a teen's first introduction to alcohol happens in the home or through a family member.

### Availability in the Home

When alcohol or other drugs are available in the home, it is accessible to the teen. Often liquor and wine are not locked up, and when they are, it usually isn't difficult for a teen to figure out how to gain access, which becomes a big temptation for the teen when the parents are out of the home. Alcohol in the home is best locked up, closely monitored, and used discreetly and prudently by adults.

### Social Role Models and Media Advertising

Teens are tuned in to what others around them are doing and to what's "cool," and some teens will drink to fit in. Patterns of this type of use often correspond to fads and involve noticeable lifestyle changes, including type of music, going to parties or concerts, or dressing, grooming, and behaving like a selected role model.

### Poor Refusal Skills

Teens who lack refusal skills, the ability to say no to peer pressure, frequently succumb to pressure to drink while involved in social activities. Assertiveness skills can be taught and learned, but it usually takes more than a parent's scolding or simply saying, "Get a backbone." Refusal skills need to be developed. Some community institutions that serve youth have helpful programs that teach these in a peer-social setting, but families are also important institutions for this type of training. I remember my mother saying to me when I was a young teenager: "Stephen, if you ever find yourself in a car with friends who start drinking or doing something wrong, I want you to get out of that car immediately. If you have to, call me and I'll come and get you no matter where you are." And my unspoken thought was: "Ah, Mom, I can't do that. That would make me look stupid. I can take care of myself." The truth was, I couldn't take care of myself, and I wasn't good at saying no to peer pressure. That came later. Nevertheless, that comment by my mother reinforced in me the importance of character, and if nothing else, I knew what she valued, and that mattered to me. But assertiveness skills need to be taught, and they come with an emotional realization that we have a right to and can say no to dangerous things and that being true to ourselves and true principles is more important than being true to a friend who is leading us into dangerous or destructive paths. This kind of power comes when a teen gains self-esteem and an inner sense of worth and identity.

### Inadequate Supervision

Inadequate parental supervision provides opportunity for boredom and poor use of unstructured time. Supervision is not to be confused with control. Rather, supervision has to do with attention, monitoring, communication, influence, persuasion, and respectful guidance. Parents who know their kids know when things change in their kids' lives and moods; they are more able to respond, to set clear standards and expectations, and then to monitor and supervise their children. For the most part, parents who do this find less potential for rebellion or dangerous wandering and can significantly reduce the risk for teen alcohol use.

*Permissiveness and Lack of Rules*

Teens need fences and boundaries on their time, friends, and activities. Giving in to teens' demands or wants for certain activities often puts them at the wrong place at the wrong time with the wrong people. Parental permissiveness often comes from fear; being too busy, too overwhelmed, or too tired to act; selfishness; or neglect for whatever reason. According to noted religious leader Gordon B. Hinckley, "Permissiveness never produced greatness. Integrity, loyalty and strength are virtues whose sinews are developed through the struggles that go on within a [youth] as he practices self-discipline."

Lack of rules leaves children uncertain or confused about exact standards, values, and expectations. Rules act as fences. Rules serve as a strength upon which a child can rely when peer pressure mounts outside the direct care of parents. A child can always say, "I'm not allowed to." As parents, we need to avoid merely enforcing rules. That makes us a sheriff instead of a coach, always apprehending and ticketing, instead of guiding. It's easier and more productive to be a coach. We empower our teen to be her own sheriff. We need to enforce the rule but also to teach the deeper principle behind the rule by living it and talking to our teen about it. When our teen needs a time-out, we can take her out of the game for a time, rather than yelling at her as she runs up and down the court of life. We can compliment her on her efforts, give her specific pointers on her mistakes, and provide suggestions on improvement. Principles convey love and respect and confidence. Rules convey control. Both are necessary. But rebellion comes when only rules are enforced without the teaching of the principle. We need to be a teacher, not an enforcer only.

Stephen R. Covey taught two principles necessary to motivating teens from within: involving the teen in the problem and establishing a sense of trust.[3] The first principle helps our teen feel a sense of responsibility, of being a part of the solution, instead of just the problem. The second opens the door for our child to be trained in what he should do, to be committed to it, and to receive our help.

## Environmental Factors

### Attitudes That Support or Promote Alcohol Use

Attitudes that recklessly promote alcohol use invite teens to adopt the same attitudes. I worked with a fourteen-year-old from Texas whose father and grandfather believed that to be a "real" man, you had to go to bars, drink, and fight anyone who got in your way. They taught him that he was a wimp if he didn't do that. That boy didn't have the temperament to be a brawling drinker. He liked poetry and art. The distress of these ingrained, yet incompatible values caused him to fail in school and get into trouble. Parents, consider your attitudes, including those about alcohol.

Teens who come from families or communities that wink at or tolerate drinking or misbehavior may be more prone to abuse alcohol. It is unfair to wink at teenage drinking and punish adult alcoholic behavior, or to wink at a teenager driving under the influence but prosecute one who tragically has an accident and kills someone. These are double standards that mislead teens into thinking that there is nothing harmful or dangerous about drinking until something serious happens. I found this double standard while I served in the military years ago. Alcohol was a prized social ingredient. Drinking was something everyone did. Men lived for happy hour. The clubs were the popular places. Unit social parties were beer parties. Even official dining events were unthinkable without wine, followed by a ranking officer announcing, "The bar is open." Yet base commanders took a dim view on anyone caught driving under the influence or involved in domestic violence. Many careers of good men and women were ruined because alcohol was encouraged, even promoted, and then condemned when taken to excess. Promoting and punishing alcohol use is a double standard.

## Nonconformity

Teens who value independence and not conforming with social norms, rules, and expectations are more likely to partake of alcohol. This often takes the form of disobedience or rebellion or belligerence, an attitude that "no one has the right to tell me what to do or to control my life." This is a learned behavior from key role models in teens' lives, beginning with their parents, siblings, and other relatives. It is a value learned through television and film characters and from peer groups. For teens, one way to demonstrate nonconformity is to do things that are not allowed at their age, such as drinking.

## Lack of Clear Values and Standards Consistent with Sobriety

Two problems with values may induce children to try alcohol: (1) the absence of values that teach a healthy sense of right and wrong relating to alcohol use, and (2) misguided values that condone the use of alcohol or other risky behavior. Our children need to know that we value positive, healthy behaviors that are consistent with laws of society. Failure to teach and enforce solid values and standards of living regarding behavior and alcohol abuse is like sending them out to battle without weapons or protection. Values are statements of beliefs that are held as significant to the family. Values that create disharmony between fundamental family and social rules place adolescents in conflict. Standards are symbols or tokens of the values that a family or society honors. Standards are visible symbols for teens. A family's values are reflected in their standards of dress, grooming, language, and behavior. Parents can set and require standards in the home that are consistent with positive values and teach their children to have the courage to abide by these standards.

## Low Socioeconomic Status

Studies suggest that social, economic, and environmental factors are even more influential than genetics in promoting or delaying the drinking of alcohol by teens. I do not mean to imply that people who are not as wealthy or privileged as others are lesser parents or that they are more prone to abuse alcohol. A home and a family—no matter how humble—that is run with love and devotion and sound values has the power to raise strong, productive children. I do mean that circumstances—often beyond parents' control—can increase the risk for teens to come into contact with alcohol. Children whose opportunities for better education, social experiences, and relationships are inhibited by social or economic status appear to be at greater risk for discouragement, boredom, and delinquency that can lead to alcohol and other drug use.

## Legal Attitudes about Alcohol

Alcohol use by teens is promoted when the laws pertaining to underage alcohol abuse are not clear or when they are not enforced by police or consistently adjudicated by juvenile court judges. Teens need consistent and firm consequences at the outset of their drinking, and when such consequences are applied, teens have a good chance of avoiding further problems.

## Financial Resources

Teens who have money from their parents or an older sibling to buy alcohol or who have their own unsupervised bank accounts are at higher risk for buying and using alcohol. Kids with liberal privileges, unsupervised access to cars, and other benefits are often attracted to people who drink and to activities where alcohol is served. Money, position, and privilege can break down healthy barriers and make a teen more at risk for problems.

## Why Do Some Teens Persist in Abusing Alcohol?

Persistent teenage use of alcohol is not moderate or controlled. Statistics show that when drinking starts early—at age thirteen to fifteen—and persists, as many as 42 percent of these kids will have drinking problems. Not all early drinkers drop off the deep end of abuse and plunge into self-destruction. Drinking for some remains unnoticeable and unobtrusive for the most part; others quit altogether. But for many, life becomes a series of domestic, financial, legal, and social problems. People who prevent or postpone the use of alcohol until they are beyond the impulsive years of adolescence—beyond twenty-one years of age—are much less likely to be problem drinkers. The longer the abstinence prior to onset of drinking is, the lower the probability of problem drinking.[4] Following are some reasons a teen might persist in abusing alcohol.

### Absence of Consequences

Teens who do not experience early or consistent consequences for drinking have little impetus to stop drinking, especially if they like it and are getting social perks. It is human tendency not to make needed changes until undesirable consequences are felt—a form of operant conditioning. The natural consequences of problem drinking—addiction or serious abuse—can be punishing to teens. Some come sooner, some later, but they come, and as they do, the person grows out of adolescence into adulthood where the expectations are higher and the tolerance for problem conduct is lower. Early consequences of addiction and problem abuse are school failure, family conflict, legal and social problems, and loss of trust, confidence, and respect from others. Persistent alcohol abuse often brings on injury, accidents, death of friends, sexually transmitted and other diseases, and unwanted pregnancies. Long-term consequences include family and marriage failures, loss of jobs or inability to find or retain good employment, more serious disease, and perhaps imprisonment. When parents, school authorities, and church and community leaders unite to impose undesirable consequences for drinking and provide positive alternatives to drinking, teens will be less likely to continue to drink.

## Rewards

Teens who continue to abuse alcohol despite knowing that they are breaking the law and placing themselves at risk are getting some reward from their behavior that is stronger than the negatives. It may be a social or emotional reward, or it may be a craving for alcohol driven by dependence. Lashing out at the unwanted behavior without looking for the underlying motivation for the behavior is like hacking at the leaves instead of striking at the root. Parents will need to find and resolve the deeper need that is causing the alcohol abuse or misbehavior. We cannot and should not do this by ourselves; it usually requires professional help, especially when deeper psychological or addiction issues are at play. Almost every community has access to professional counselors, therapists, psychologists, psychiatrists, and other care programs that can help.

## Ignorance

Lack of proper knowledge about alcohol and addiction can cause both parents and teens to continue to use alcohol. Teens may continue using alcohol and reject any adult or sober peer pressure to stop because they have false beliefs based on wrong information. Teens who use alcohol often have a lot of street information about their drug of choice, but usually not many clear facts. They justify and rationalize their use with their selected bits of information. Most teens, especially those in the younger and middle teen years (twelve to sixteen), have not developed strong logical reasoning capacities, since the reasoning part of the brain is usually not fully developed until they reach seventeen or eighteen years of age. The continued abuse of alcohol reinforces faulty thinking.

## Role Modeling

Teens from families that actively drink and condone drinking among family members may receive strong support to continue drinking, in spite of any outside social pressure to refrain. A teen also gets support for using from peer groups. Sports figures and other celebrities who drink can be strong advocates for the teen to drink. It becomes the cool thing to do. Strong values and a sense of self-worth in a teen can minimize the influence of outside role models.

## Dependence or Addiction

A teen will continue to use alcohol as long as the craving continues. Addiction to alcohol creates a primarily physical dependence upon the drug, producing a craving for it. The cravings ignite rationalization, justification, and wishful thinking that perpetuate the abuse in a vicious downward spiral. More will be said about this in chapter 4.

Alcoholism is not a problem that develops in a vacuum. A child grows up in a system of forces that make him either at risk for or resistant to the problems of alcohol abuse and addiction. There are many forces at work in a child's life, and parents are empowered to play an active and useful role in recognizing and defusing high-risk precipitators of alcoholism. We each have different circumstances, it is true, but happily there are correct principles that each of us can apply in our lives, to the best of our abilities, which can bring about positive results in helping our children live happier, more productive lives without the influence of alcohol.

# Chapter 4

# Alcohol Addiction: Is There Such a Thing as Responsible Teenage Drinking?

There is no such thing as responsible teenage drinking of alcohol. That is a misnomer because, first, teens, alcohol, and responsibility don't go well together. Second, even if teens don't drink to excess, it is illegal for them to use, thus making it irresponsible in social terms.

Not every teen who drinks is going to become an alcoholic or even have major problems with alcohol abuse. A majority of teens who try alcohol will experiment and then either abandon its use altogether or wait until they are of legal age and then use socially or moderately. However, a significant number—14 million, or 1 out of 13—will get into trouble with alcohol abuse or become addicted. When teens sustain a complete loss of control over alcohol use, they have crossed the line and reached a condition known as dependence, addiction, or alcoholism.

**What Exactly Is Abuse?**

From a legal and responsible point of view, any use of alcohol by someone under the age of twenty-one is abuse. It's against the law. From a clinical point of view, abuse is using controlled substances for purposes for which the drug was not prescribed or in ways that are potentially harmful to the person, without medical reason or supervision. Doctors don't prescribe alcoholic beverages to help us feel better (although some medications do contain alcohol).

Abuse can be correctly viewed as potentially a beginning phase of dependence, starting with misuse and turning into persistent abuse. Abuse of alcohol should be a real reason for concern in parents, in part, because the line between addiction and abuse can be very thin and easily stepped across, especially for a teen.

To be considered substance abuse, one or more of the following four criteria, established by the American Psychiatric Association, must have occurred in a person's life within a twelve-month period.

1. *Failure to fulfill major responsibilities and expectations at home, school, or work.* In the home, for instance, an abusing teen might become negligent in completing assigned chores or even become belligerent; he may start missing family meals or special family events; become more withdrawn or isolated or stay in his room when at home; or become hurtful and argumentative with younger siblings, frightening them with violence or anger and disappointing them with failed promises and seeming disregard. At school, the teen often exhibits truancy, tardiness, falling grades, failed tests, uncompleted assignments, and a general disinterest. He may stop associating with his classmates or drop out of sports or extracurricular activities that were once of high interest. He may even demonstrate conflict with schoolmates and authority. If he has a part-time job, he may lose it or quit for no apparent reason.

2. *Drinking in situations that are physically dangerous to self or others.* Usually for teens, this is mostly manifested in relationship to cars or other social settings. Parents typically don't know about these situations unless the teen is caught or has an accident and it is brought to their attention. Acts that are physically dangerous, of course, include driving a car under the influence

of alcohol, riding in a car driven by someone under the influence, and performing dangerous acts with a car on public streets, such as racing, careening, or harassing other drivers. Sometimes teens will perform other dangerous acts under the influence, such as climbing on high or dangerous places, playing chicken with trains, or performing other stunts to show off. But danger goes beyond the physical; it includes serious emotional dangers. Often, a reckless physical act brings on profound emotional pain, such as an accident that causes serious injury to or the death of another person, whether a friend or a stranger. These events change a teen's life forever. Sometimes teens under the influence will place themselves in danger of physical violence and criminal actions, such as brawls, fights, or gang fights.

3. *Recurrent substance-related legal problems*. Often problems with teen alcoholism play out in legal conflicts. A teen typically begins by being apprehended with alcohol, perhaps in a car or at a party; the problems may increase to more serious behaviors such as malicious trespassing, breaking and entering, assaults, breaking curfews, theft and grand theft auto, even armed robbery. This is typically related to teens trying to get money to finance their abuse or being with peers who are involved in such behavior. Slaps on the wrist turn into tickets and probation, then into court appearances, heavier fines, juvenile detention, work farms, treatment centers, and eventually prison.

4. *Continuing to use despite recurring or worsening social or interpersonal problems*. Alcohol abuse can permeate all parts of children's lives. They don't hide it well, and it is evident to the most casual observer. Abusing teens will persist in drinking in spite of increasing problems. Sometimes it seems as if they

don't care or are oblivious to what is happening to them. Often, it is because they can't admit that they've lost control. Performance in school declines, problems with police and juvenile officials persist, family dysfunction worsens, and every aspect of their lives seems to be on a downward spiral, but they cling to drinking and being with their drinking friends like passengers on the *Titanic* clinging to a guardrail until they are completely submerged.

## What Exactly Is Addiction?

Addiction to alcohol, referred to also as alcoholism, has been defined as a disease of the body and mind that results in physical, social, emotional, and mental deterioration and that eventually ends in moral and spiritual bankruptcy. A dictionary definition of *disease* is "an illness or a particular destructive process in an organism, or change in the body from its normal or healthy state, with specific causes and characteristic symptoms." A disease can be aggressive and fast acting, or it can be less aggressive. It can be seriously debilitating and fatal, or it can be benign.

Alcoholism, like other forms of addiction, is properly called a disease because it successfully meets this definition. Alcoholism has specific causes, symptoms, treatment protocols, and outcomes. It can be prevented. It can occur rapidly or take a long time to progress, depending upon the individual. It has no ethnic, gender, age, economic, educational, or social status boundaries. It can strike anyone, although some people are at higher risk.

Alcoholism, as with any other addiction, has the following seven primary symptoms, as identified by the American Psychiatric Association. At least three of these must be present in order to qualify for a diagnosis of dependence, or addiction.

*Tolerance* is the need to drink greater amounts of alcohol in order to get high or drunk. With the onset of alcoholism, the teen's body begins to adjust and tolerate the alcohol, and it will require more and stronger alcohol to get the same intoxication as before. Typical symptoms include the teen drinking more at one time and more frequently, shifting to drinks with greater alcohol percentages, or combining alcohol with other drugs (polysubstance abuse), or even shifting from alcohol to a more potent drug.

*Withdrawal* is the physical and emotional discomfort or pain, such as anxiety, irritation, nausea, shakiness, and sweating, that occurs when the teen stops drinking or tries to cut down. These physical and emotional discomforts are the body's reactions to not having its fix, and they can be severe, forcing the teen into more drinking to get relief. Usually the teen will try to hide these symptoms, not wanting parents or others to notice, which leaves him alone to face the insurmountable and overwhelming sensations of withdrawal. The teen will inevitably fail and succumb to drinking.

*Loss of control* is the inability to control, limit, or stop drinking. The teen may make commitments and promises to quit—often well-intended and emotional declarations of intention—but is unable to make good on them. She drinks when she didn't intend to, and she drinks until drunk. She gulps and drains drinks, instead of sipping and enjoying. Her life becomes out of balance and driven by a need for alcohol.

*Lifestyle changes* become evident in appearance, language, behaviors, relationships, habits, interests, and even music. Alcoholism causes major changes in a teen's lifestyle. Dress, grooming, and personal care often drop off significantly or in noticeable ways; interests and hobbies change to activities surrounding alcohol and alcohol culture. A teen may give up sports or a special talent to hang out with friends. The people, places, and things in his life begin to focus on alcohol. He may become more isolated from the positive, normal aspects of society and family.

*Continued use despite worsening problems* means that the teen will persist in drinking alcohol even when it is obviously the cause of significant relationship and behavioral problems. Denial of problems, avoidance of withdrawal pains, and the craving for alcohol are stronger than the desire to quit or gain control. Many teenage alcoholics have lost all hope and do not anticipate reaching adulthood.

*Preoccupation* means that the teen spends most of her time preoccupied with alcohol: thinking about it, trying to get it, drinking, or overcoming the aftereffects of the drunk. The driving force behind this obsession with alcohol is the intense craving for it. Little time is left for anything else in life.

*Increased use of drugs* means that the teen uses more alcohol, more frequently, more intensely. He may begin to mix alcohol with other drugs, which becomes extremely dangerous. Alcohol is known as a gateway drug, meaning that it is an entry drug that can lead to other illicit drug use, such as amphetamines, methamphetamine, hallucinogens, and other depressants.

Alcoholism is caused by the use or abuse of alcohol and the body's resultant dependence upon it; it's that simple. If left untreated, alcoholism will result in the deterioration of the body, mind, intellect, social life, and spirit of the victim.

### Crossing the Line

There are three potential causes of addiction:

1. Genetic inheritance. Alcoholic teens may have inherited from their biological parents the genes that make them especially susceptible to alcohol dependence. Once they begin to drink, that genetic link is activated to cause a rapid development of addiction. Studies show that biological children of parents who are alcoholic or those with a history of alcoholism

in the family are at higher risk, perhaps as much as ten times higher than children without such a family history.

2. Sustained use. The alcohol or other substance being abused may be powerful enough or taken into the body in sufficient quantities and for a long enough time that the body becomes dependent upon the substance. Methamphetamine, a synthetically produced stimulant drug produced in clandestine labs and known as meth, crank, crystal meth, and speed, is a prime example. Methamphetamine has the capacity to permanently disrupt and change the nervous system, thus changing the way a person thinks, perceives, feels, and behaves for long periods of time, perhaps even for the rest of her life. Alcohol does not normally wield that kind of immediate power, but it can cause disabling dependence if taken in sufficient quantities over extended periods of time.

3. Environmental factors. It is now believed that a teen's environment—his social and cultural setting, family environment, school setting, and stresses and pressures—can actually induce or promote the development of alcoholism.

When alcohol is consumed under any of these three circumstances, a body can become physically dependent upon the presence of alcohol to feel normal. When alcohol is not present in sufficient quantities, the teen's body begins to crave alcohol. Usually, it is not just a craving for a little alcohol but for the feeling of being drunk or high. Serious abusers and alcoholics almost always drink until they are drunk. The craving controls and diminishes all other human functions, and the presence of alcohol in high enough quantities prevents the performance of normal daily responsibilities and causes disease, accident, serious injury, and misbehaviors. Depending upon the person, it can also result in loss of emotional control and abusive behavior to family and others.

We may question the reality of teenage addiction. We may believe that it is an adult disease and that it takes a long time to become addicted to alcohol. We may see our child's drinking as merely a passing fancy, and for some it may well be. But the sad reality is that teenagers do become addicted to alcohol, even at very young (pre-adolescent) ages, and addiction can happen quickly, as rapidly as a few months, depending upon the teen and her environment. Some alcoholics insist that they knew they were dependent the moment they took their first drink.

It is worth stating again that the younger people are when they start drinking, the more likely they are to develop alcohol dependence.

## Won't It Just Go Away?

Wouldn't it be great if this disease of alcoholism were like a virus or a cold and would just go away after a while? Wouldn't it be nice if the body could somehow just overcome the disease and wake up one morning feeling better? It doesn't work that way with alcoholism. The longer alcohol is used by an alcoholic, the more severe the problems and consequences become.

The craving for alcohol does not become active within a person until alcohol activates it, but once it is active, it will progress and worsen in a predictable, observable pattern over time. Its normal steps of progression are shown below. Not all the steps are always observable in the life of an addicted teen, but this presents a realistic view of the process.

### Progression

At first our teen may experiment, trying alcohol out of curiosity or because of peer pressure. The more available the alcohol and the stronger the influence from people a teen values, the greater is the possibility that she'll try it. She doesn't intend to use a lot; she just wants to try it. This is the *experimentation* phase. If she finds it to be enjoyable, fun, exciting, or helpful in some way, she may decide that it is "cool."

A teen may continue to experiment with alcohol. He doesn't drink regularly, perhaps not even frequently, but his attitude about alcohol is changing. He is beginning to believe that alcohol isn't harmful, as his parents or other adults have told him, but that it's fun and exciting and opens up a new world of friendships. He may even like the taste. This is the stage of *misuse*. In other words, alcohol isn't being used for its intended purpose or it is being used in excess. This phase is especially critical if our teen is also suffering from other problems or trauma in his life and is seeking expression or relief through the use of alcohol. It is in this stage that he gives himself over to alcohol; his attitudes and belief systems change at this point.

Our teen increases her drug use, making excuses for use and denying any guilt feelings or problems that are beginning to crop up at home, in school, or in the community. She begins to change friends, activities, and the places she goes. She begins to compromise her values and may give up beliefs or interest in spiritual endeavors. She begins to have legal, behavioral, and emotional problems, but she refuses to see them as problems that she wants to solve. The alcohol has taken control by now, and she is using even when she doesn't really want to, although she remains in denial by saying that she can quit anytime she wants to; she just doesn't want to quit right now. She is in the *abuse* phase.

In the *dependence* phase, or alcoholism, alcohol has now taken over the body and will. A teen needs regular doses and more of it just to maintain equilibrium. His body does not feel normal without drinking alcohol, and he is subjected to severe craving. He experiences severe withdrawal symptoms when he tries to quit or cut back. This is a frightening time for our teen, a time when he feels trapped and discouraged. He may realize that alcohol is bad for him and he may wish to quit, but can't. He may try several times to quit or cut down. He may make promises to himself, close friends, or even family members, but he is unable to successfully keep them. Furthermore, his behaviors have caused conflict at home, at school, and with others, so his support system is rapidly slipping away.

The *addiction* phase is marked by the symptoms of dependence, but now our teen begins a path of amoral behavior and spiritual bankruptcy. She has compromised her values and standards completely, losing the spiritual light of basic human decency that once shone in her. She will do anything for alcohol, even commit violent crimes. As a teen, she may not have access to much money, so she must find her drug funding from other sources. She may even turn to drug trafficking, robbery, and prostitution. The positive aspects of her past life—school, family relations, love, trust, friendships, beliefs and values, and past interests—have been given up for alcohol. Even her freedom is sacrificed as she spends time in juvenile detention or treatment rehabilitation. She makes promises to quit or cut back, but can't. She spends almost all of her time looking for, using, or recovering from alcohol's effects. She feels frightened, confused, and hopeless.

### A Chronic Disease

The disease of alcoholism is *chronic*, that is, persistent. It does not go away with time, like a headache or upset stomach. It is not something that a teen's immune system can eventually overcome and throw off. It will not get better without action being taken—specifically abstinence from alcohol. In fact, alcoholism remains with the victim throughout life. It need not remain active, but it remains within a former drinker and can be activated by the reintroduction of alcohol or other mood-altering drugs into his system or even by experiences and events that regenerate alcoholic feelings and thoughts.

This *chronicity* is often misunderstood by parents and teens, and they think that after a period of sobriety, they can return to controlled social drinking. This is not true. An alcoholic will always be an alcoholic—either active or in abstention. Alcohol—a psychoactive drug—will *always* have the power to resurrect a recurrence of the disease within someone who has been addicted. Alcoholism actively returns when an alcoholic begins to drink (or use other mood-altering drugs) again, and it returns with an even stronger force than it had before.

### Deadly Disease

If left untreated, alcoholism can take a teen's life by disease, accident, violence, overdose, or suicide. Many addicted teens never expect to live beyond age twenty. They give up on trying to make anything of themselves. There is a common saying around recovery circles that substance addiction tends to lead to only three possible ends: prison, the morgue, or recovery. Let me restate an important point: not every alcoholic is dying or in troubled situations. There are what is called "maintenance alcoholics" in the world who hold jobs and are good, law-abiding people, but drink every day out of necessity. In my experience, this doesn't describe the typical teenage alcoholic. Maintenance alcoholics tend to be people of an older generation who have learned how to balance their lives in spite of drinking. Teens are typically more out of control and unable to balance or manage their lives.

It is encouraging to note that alcohol-related crimes, such as burglary, robbery, assault, violent crimes, rape, and vehicular manslaughter—anything performed under the influence of or related to the consumption of alcohol—in the United States decreased significantly between the 1980s and the late 1990s, as did per capita alcohol consumption and alcohol-related traffic crashes. Yet researchers report that violent offenders in state prisons increasingly report having used alcohol prior to an offense.[1]

Drinking alcohol can be fatal for a teen, even the first time around. Many are victims of car accidents; others are maimed or killed in other types of accidents as a result of thoughtless, dangerous behavior. Teens are also killed in homicides because they are in the wrong place at the wrong time with the wrong people doing wrong things. Hundreds of teens are killed annually because of alcohol poisoning and beer bonging (pouring alcohol directly into the stomach using a rubber hose). Teens commit suicide because of the hopelessness of addiction or problems related to alcohol. Less significant, but still a factor to consider, are the teens who experience cancer, cirrhosis of the liver, heart disease, AIDS, and hepatitis because of drinking. Alcohol abuse not only harms the body; it also presents threats from the environment that can be of equal danger.

## A Disease of the System

Alcoholism is not a solitary disease, especially when it involves a teen. It affects the entire system. Perhaps a teen believes that "it is her right to do what she wants as long as it doesn't hurt anyone else." These behaviors and attitudes are sometimes wrongly referred to as "victimless crimes" because we convince ourselves that they don't hurt anyone but ourselves. Not so with teen alcoholism. A teen's misbehaviors will directly or indirectly affect her family, friends, neighbors, community, school, and nation.

From surveys and studies done by the Pacific Institute for Research and Evaluation, the cost of underage drinking to the nation is estimated to total more than $58 billion per year.[2] In 1992, the estimated productivity loss for employees with a past or current history of alcoholism was nearly $67 billion.[3] Kids grow up to be employees.

The system from which our teen comes is responsible for creating or sustaining the problem of alcohol abuse. This is not to say that our teen doesn't share responsibility for his or her actions and decisions.

But families, communities, and social institutions also need to take responsibility for actions that influence and shape a teen's beliefs, attitudes, behaviors, and relationships about alcohol use. Perhaps we've heard the saying "It takes a village to raise a child." So much of what our children do is learned and mimicked behavior coming from our families, friends, schools, and other social institutions. Our children are attuned to what we and others do more than what we say. A collective belief system in a community has extreme power upon the values and beliefs of our teen, and ultimately influences his behavior.

On one occasion, I was invited to meet with a school district staff to train them on the *Adolescent Recovery Plan*, a curriculum that I had written for Hazelden. In preparation for the trip, I asked the director what precipitating concerns had occasioned the invitation. I found it interesting that teachers and administrators were seeking training in treating children with alcohol and other drug problems. Normally, schools counsel and educate, but refer treatment to professionals. The response was, "Abuse and addiction to alcohol and other drugs by teens in our community has become intolerable and is jeopardizing the education of the children, and nobody seems to care or is willing to do anything about it, so we're forced to take matters into our own hands." In my discussions with the teachers, I found that children were living in homes with parents who were abusing or addicted and in communities that fostered such abuse as normal, and community leaders were doing nothing about it. In fact, during our two-day training, an incident of overdose happened right on the steps of the school one morning. An entire generation of young people was being brought up in a drug and alcohol culture.

## The Impact of Addiction on Growth

Youth is a time for growth—physical, emotional, spiritual, intellectual, and social. Addiction could strike at no worse time because it stunts and prevents critical development and devours important experiences and opportunities. Some of these, if lost during adolescence, cannot be recovered. Entire textbooks have been devoted to this topic, and I cannot hope to cover all the details within the scope of this book. However, let's review some of the key areas.

### Physical and Cognitive Growth

We have noted researchers' belief that alcohol abuse can hinder the development of bone in our teen's skeletal growth, leaving it weakened and underdeveloped. It can also damage the development of major organs, such as the heart, brain, lungs, and liver. Scientific findings imply that chronic alcohol use can damage cells and hormones in the male's reproductive system and can even affect the health of offspring.[4] Research suggests that normal timing and progression of puberty may be at risk in adolescents consuming even relatively moderate amounts of alcohol on a regular basis. Alcohol can delay puberty, which can affect a child's sense of self-esteem and social acceptability.[5] Chronic alcohol abuse can influence a teen's development of rational and complex thinking and problem-solving skills. Relatively simple problems can seem overwhelming when a teen has not learned to think through and deal both emotionally and cognitively with challenges because he has learned to avoid problems by simply drinking or getting high.

### Social and Emotional Growth

Addiction to alcohol or other drugs can significantly retard a teen's social and emotional growth. Relationships are often forfeited to abuse drugs, and the relationships that do exist are frequently drug-dependent. Often, children develop codependent relationships that are dysfunctional associations based upon needs and weaknesses instead of strengths and abilities to establish positive boundaries and associations. A love-trust relationship builds with the drug to the exclusion of all other relationships that interfere with the addiction, leaving the youth stunted in his ability to bring positive gifts to someone else and to be able to establish positive emotional bonding. Often such children have not learned to cope with and control their emotions except through chemical manipulations. Frequently, such children become involved in dangerous and inappropriate sexual relationships through alcohol or other drugs, leaving them open to AIDS, the hepatitis C virus, and other sexually transmitted diseases. Some girls are raped or taken advantage of or sell their bodies for drugs or illusory relationships.

### Communication Skills

Addiction can stunt a teen's ability to properly relate with others and to communicate her needs effectively. Opportunities to develop in these areas through school and extracurricular activities are often lost because the teen is off drinking and doing other drugs. Sometimes these drinking relationships can be fairly base and primitive in their scope, which further distances the teen from the mainstream of life. Her ability to talk through or communicate her needs and concerns is often stunted because she has learned to drink away problems or hide them in a bottle, so to speak.

### Life Skills

Addiction can prevent a teen from learning important life skills and ways to take care of himself. His time and effort is preoccupied with finding and using alcohol, to the exclusion of learning and experiencing other things. He may develop poor habits of nutrition, sleeping, dress, and grooming. He probably will not learn to act responsibly toward others and will not be able to fulfill age-appropriate responsibilities and tasks. He may not learn job skills—finding, holding, and excelling in a job. He may miss out on important education, knowledge, and other skills that would make him competitive in the adult world of work and living.

Many older teens I have worked with had really lost out on much of their normal teenage life. Some should have been preparing for high school graduation but were still freshmen or sophomores. Some had lost out on opportunities to play high school sports, some even with professional talent, but they couldn't qualify to play because they didn't meet the academic and behavior standards insisted upon by the school and the coach, or they simply couldn't compete with sober kids. Some had lost out on proms, graduations, and other important events because they were in detention or treatment. Many had failed to develop the social, intellectual, and life skills needed for successful entry into adulthood. Life just seemed to have passed them by, and many of them deeply regretted it once they became clean and sober. Below, I've provided examples of the losses sustained by kids who seriously abuse or are addicted to alcohol.

- Missing out on important family activities and relationships
- Falling behind in school and learning opportunities
- Missing out on sports or other opportunities to use special talents or skills
- Loss of healthy talents, interests, and leisure opportunities
- Poor development of emotional, physical, and mental capacities
- Building a serious juvenile delinquency or criminal record
- Missing out on positive friendships; being excluded by the healthy kids
- Spending significant periods of time in treatment centers or programs
- Unable to sustain consistency of emotional stability
- Loss of balance of priorities in life

### Are Addicted Teens Just Bad Apples?

Do teens act badly because they drink alcohol, or do they drink alcohol because they are acting badly? Some people believe that teenage alcoholics are just bad apples—immoral, undisciplined, weak-willed kids with character flaws. Some communities and legal systems still approach alcoholism with this view, applying swift and stern punishment. An article in *Newsweek*, dated November 25, 2002, stated: "It is worrisome that society is medicalizing more and more behavioral problems, often defining as addictions what earlier, sterner generations explained as weakness of will. Prodded by science, or what purports to be science, society is reclassifying what once were considered character flaws or moral failings as personality disorders akin to physical disabilities."

There are important truths for parents in this statement. It is not to our advantage to excuse weak wills, lack of discipline and values, and character flaws in the name of some medical condition or to try to find a medical solution to a problem best solved by limit setting and self-discipline. Nevertheless, alcoholism is a disease, not a lack of willpower. Not experimenting with alcohol in the first place would have required some willpower, it's true. But an adolescent usually doesn't see experimentation as a lack of willpower but as satisfying his natural, and often healthy, curiosity. Telling a child to "shape up," to "stop acting like a jerk," or to "get a backbone instead of a wishbone" does not stop the physical craving for alcohol that often drives the antisocial behavior. Putting teens in juvenile detention and penitentiaries only serves to worsen the problem. We need to clearly separate the inherent worth of the child from the horror of the addiction and the addictive behaviors.

Teens who are abusing alcohol or suffering from alcoholism may behave badly. They may steal, lie, burglarize, vandalize, commit crimes, and commit violent acts while under the influence of alcohol or to get alcohol. A girl once told me that she robbed gas stations and convenience stores for liquor. She was terrified of getting caught, but she wanted the alcohol more than she feared the consequences.

While alcoholism is sometimes manifested in self-defeating and troublesome behavior, in terms of treating alcoholism, the behavior is more a leaf than a root of the problem. Alcoholism is caused by the body's dependence upon alcohol, not by bad behavior. Admittedly, there are teens who have antisocial personalities who also abuse alcohol, but recovery from alcoholism cannot be won by merely controlling behavior, only by dealing with the craving and the self-destruction of an addicted teen. For example, stopping a teen from stealing to support his drinking habit will not stop the craving for alcohol; however, treating the alcohol dependence will change the behavior. Instead of trying to remove the person out of the slum, so to speak, we should remove the slum out of the person. Then, they will take themselves out of the slum.

### What about Psychological Problems?

Some experts argue that alcoholics have an underlying emotional or psychological problem. For instance, a teen might suffer from major depression, antisocial personality traits, defiance, or other adjustment or mood problems that bring her to drink and become abusive with alcohol or another drug. The implication is that if we can resolve the underlying psychological problem, the drinking problem can be solved. We must remember that alcoholism is *caused* by a physical dependence on alcohol. While some psychological problems can put a child at high risk for the abuse of alcohol, and while such problems often worsen the effects of abuse and addiction, they don't cause alcoholism. For example, a teen who is discouraged because of school failure or other problems might be inclined to begin drinking and hanging out with kids who drink, but it's alcohol that addicts the body, not the teen's discouragement. A teen who has difficulty controlling strong emotions might turn to drinking to try to cope with the problems. The emotions may give rise to the abuse, but they don't cause dependence. When psychological problems are coupled with drug addiction, a person is said to have co-occurring or dual disorders. It is not uncommon for a teen to be addicted to more than one drug or to have more than one psychological problem, such as depression and attention deficit disorder. Alcoholism can mimic psychological symptoms, such as mood shifts, depression, anger, or mental problems, making it difficult for parents and professionals alike to recognize the source of a teen's problem. Addiction and a psychological problem can exacerbate each other, but neither problem will be resolved without being specifically treated for its needs. Treating the psychological problem may lessen the risk factor but will not resolve the craving for alcohol. Without treating the craving for alcohol, the teen may be at risk for returning to psychological problems. Likewise, treating the addiction without treating the psychological problem will leave the teen at very high risk for relapse into alcohol abuse.

**Who's Responsible?**
More recently, the view has been put forward that alcoholism is a specific disease, much like chickenpox, asthma, or diabetes. This view has helped considerably in eliminating the damaging stigma of the past and has given addiction useful emphasis in treatment. However, two dangers arise from a purely medical model.

First, it is not to anyone's advantage to excuse responsibility for damaging and dangerous behavior associated with addiction by simply absolving someone of any responsibility. Second, as mentioned before, it is not effective to treat the addiction and ignore the related social, emotional, psychological, family, spiritual, and behavioral issues. True recovery must deal with all.

The point I wish to make here is that teenage alcoholism is a disease that embodies all of the views stated above, but true alcoholism is caused by one thing only: the body's physical dependence upon alcohol. That must be dealt with specifically, along with the broader range of problems that put a teen at risk, if we are to be successful in preventing, diverting, and treating alcoholism in teens.

We must hold each other and our teen appropriately accountable if she is going to grow up to be a productive, responsible adult. But what is appropriate responsibility? Let me illustrate it with the following story.

### An Ancient Tale

Long ago in an ancient kingdom there lived a princess who was very young and very beautiful. The princess, recently married, lived in a large and luxurious castle with her husband, a powerful and wealthy lord. The young princess was not content, however, to sit on her throne and eat strawberries by herself while her husband took frequent and long journeys to neighboring kingdoms. She felt neglected and soon became quite unhappy. One day, while she was alone in the castle gardens, a handsome vagabond rode out of the forest bordering the castle. He spied the beautiful princess and quickly won her heart.

Following a day of dalliance, the young princess found herself ruthlessly abandoned by the vagabond. She discovered that the only way back to the castle led through the enchanted forest of the wicked sorcerer. Fearing to venture into the forest alone, she sought out her wise and kind godfather. She explained her plight, begged his forgiveness, and asked for his assistance in returning home before her husband returned. But the godfather, shocked by her behavior, refused forgiveness and denied her any assistance.

Discouraged but still determined, the princess disguised her identity and sought the help of a noble knight of the kingdom. After hearing her sad story, the knight pledged his unfailing aid for a modest fee. But, alas, the princess had no money, and the knight rode away to save other damsels in distress.

The beautiful princess had no one else from which she could seek help and decided to brave the great peril alone. She followed the safest path she knew through the forest, but the wicked sorcerer spied her and caused her to be devoured by the fire-breathing dragon.[6]

Who is responsible for the death of the princess? Was it the princess because she made a bad decision? Was it the lord because of his insensitivity and neglect of his wife? The godfather who should have had compassion but was indignant at her behavior? The noble knight who could have saved her but wanted something for his efforts? The vagabond who put her in great peril by his selfish behavior? The wicked sorcerer who sent the dragon? Or was it the dragon that actually devoured her? A case can be made to justify and convict everyone in the cast.

The point to be made is that every life has its dragons and sorcerers and vagabonds. All of the characters in the story represent people and influences in a teen's life; each of them had some responsibility in the princess's death. The princess represents an impulsive, bored teen; the lord and the godfather represent parents or other family members; the noble knight and the godfather represent people in the community or extended family who won't help unless they get something for their efforts or withhold their help because they are judgmental; the vagabond represents peers and other social influences that entice children onto dangerous paths; the wicked sorcerer represents evil and designing people who would unscrupulously feed our children dangerous things; and the dragon represents the actual things that kill or harm our teens: guns, violence, drugs, alcohol, crime, and sexual promiscuity. Everyone plays a role.

# Chapter 5

# A Model of Adolescent Addiction: What Happens When Kids Cross the Line?

**N**ow that we've looked at alcohol as a drug, addiction as a disease, and our teen as a developing human being, let's put them together into a working model and see how they all fit together. This model also has some application for teens who are abusing alcohol but may not have crossed the line into addiction. From earlier chapters, we remember that the percentage of teenage abuse of alcohol increases by nearly 50 percent between ages fourteen and eighteen and that about 7 percent of teens (one in every thirteen) grow up to be adults with an addiction problem.

My model of teen addiction is drawn from the example of the three rocks I mentioned earlier in the book, specifically the desert marble. Teenage substance abuse, especially addiction to substances, presents itself in a similar way, although there are exceptions to this model.

### The Ring of Fire

Years ago, Johnny Cash made famous a song called "The Ring of Fire." The lyrics talk about love as a burning ring of fire into which the person fell and about how it burned. I see substance abuse and addiction as the author of these lyrics saw love: a burning ring of fire, and the farther one falls into it, the higher the flames rise and the more painful it can become.

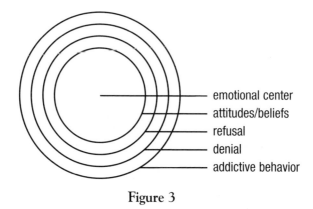

emotional center
attitudes/beliefs
refusal
denial
addictive behavior

**Figure 3**

Figure 3 is a model of teen addiction. Like the desert marble, it has a soft, inner core which we call the emotional center. Surrounding this soft emotional center is a shell, built up naturally, that serves to protect and insulate the inner emotions from the outside world.

### The Core

Our child has feelings. She is a product of her experiences thus far in life growing up in her system, a compilation of hopes and despairs, joys and sorrows, confidences and uncertainties, and losses and gains. These inner feelings are usually closely held and often not well expressed except through glimpses of the child's actions.

Even in well-adjusted teens, these feelings can include some strong and painful emotions. Addicted teens are often in greater emotional distress than their sober counterparts. Not all alcoholism evolves from serious emotional pain, and not all alcoholism provokes significant emotional upheaval. I am sure that there are some alcoholic teens who are fairly benign, uninhibited people, perhaps living out their lives relatively free from pain and conflict. However, the profile for the average alcoholic teen suggests that this is normally not the case and that he is experiencing a strong core of apprehension, self-loathing, and hopelessness caused either by the problems that arise from alcoholism or from preexisting problems that have given rise to their addiction. These inner emotions related to addiction are real, powerful, and sometimes very dangerous.

Our model of pain includes a wide band of emotions, including periods of highs and productive behavior to low periods of self-defeating activity. Many teens are fairly resilient and do not show all of the hidden fears and concerns that lie deep inside. Others can be fairly transparent and self-destructive. The stronger the pain and the less opportunity there is for healthy expression or resolution of this pain, the higher the risk for self-defeating behavior. When un-resolved pain is mixed with alcohol, the potential for serious prob-lematic abuse and eventual addiction increases. Depending on where our teen is in his course of addiction and his own sense of resiliency, he may appear anywhere along the continuum of behavior. Where does this pain come from? It's a little like asking which came first, the chicken or the egg.

### Pain-Induced Alcohol Abuse or Addiction

Life for most of us is an experience of highs and lows, joys and sorrows. Growing up in today's world isn't easy, and some decide that it isn't worth it. But most make it through and try to make of their existence a rose garden, or at least a vegetable garden. Life is filled with thorns and weeds, along with the good things.

Some children's lives get taken over by weeds that choke out the good things. Some children are led into alcohol abuse and addiction by preexisting problems that have given them a feeling of discourage-ment, rejection, unworthiness, or other emotional pain. When alco-hol is introduced, the problems may seem to subside or disappear, but it is only a temporary reprieve. They usually come back with the increased force of additional problems created by the alcohol abuse. A useful formula to explain this phenomenon is

$$\text{pain} + \text{alcohol} = \text{temporary relief} + \text{increased pain}.$$

It is not normally difficult for our teen to ask us or some other adult for help with relief from physical pain, because it is not normally tied up with a sense of self-esteem. Physical pain is just physical pain. But emotional pain is something different, something very personal. This type of pain is usually related to deeper feelings that are tied up in identity, relationships, trust, and love. So our teen is more likely to try to camouflage the pain or resolve it through self-medicating. It is equally true that our teen may not understand what is happening to her or what is causing the problem. She may struggle even to describe or recognize the actual pain.

For example, a teen struggling with learning disabilities in school and failing classes and having social conflicts with peers and teachers may get discouraged and begin using alcohol or marijuana to help him cope. He may also be vulnerable to peers who are also socially rejected and discouraged and using alcohol and other drugs.

When a parent tries to help by asking what is wrong, it may only create further frustration. Doing so requires careful and sensitive sup-port, and often the mere fact that we are the parent places us in a tumultuous situation. We often need to have help through another positive person who isn't so emotionally close to our teen but is some-one she can trust. Conflict with parents and other adults and the loss of positive peer support may exacerbate the problem and prevent her from seeking reasonable help.

If he is sufficiently hopeless, our teen may decide to turn to people, activities, and substances—such as alcohol—that help him act out the hopelessness or other feelings that he feels. He may think, *Well, I know I can never be a good student or have any good friends, so I will be the best drinker in the place. I can't please my parents or live up to their expectations, so I will abandon that hope and turn to people I can please: my drinking buddies.* Note that it is still a natural drive for acceptance or excellence; it's just twisted in a destructive manner and based on an erroneous belief system.

Where does this kind of pain come from? The sources are legion and space is too limited to speak to all of them. I will suggest a few and in brief detail.

### Lack of Self-Esteem

One of the classic voids evidenced in teens coming into treatment for substance abuse is the absence of self-worth. Sometimes this is the result of addiction and troubled behavior, and sometimes it is the result of problems that predated the addiction. High-risk kids typically have not been successful in building a sense of self-worth and value. They typically have deep inner feelings of anger, disappointment, discouragement, and loathing for themselves and others. Many of these addicted kids believe that they won't live very long and therefore don't make many long-term plans: the "eat, drink, and be merry, for tomorrow we die" philosophy.

### Lack of Self-Confidence

Some children are followers. They have not learned to trust their perceptions and decisions. Sometimes this is unintentionally conditioned into children by parents, older siblings, or others who put them down, ridicule or find fault with them, don't listen to them or give any credence to their opinions, or make all of their decisions for them. As a result, a teen may believe that she is incapable of making good decisions and may abdicate her agency by following other, more confident and powerful teens. Often this becomes the blind leading the blind.

## Negative Role Models

Children learn attitudes and beliefs from and mimic behavior of parents, siblings, peers, and social role models. Teens do what other teens do and what their heroes or role models do. They select role models who fit the image they want for themselves. The research is conclusive that negative social and peer influence promotes alcohol abuse. When children are taught that alcohol abuse is okay, they come into painful conflict with the laws and norms of society.

## Physical Roadblocks

Children who experience physical challenges that block or stunt normal growth and development of important skills are potentially at risk. Serious injuries, accidents, or long-term illnesses that disrupt normal teenage growth and development can cause feelings and needs to arise that increase the risk for alcohol and other drug abuse and addiction. Physical disabilities that prevent a teen from experiencing normal social and emotional experiences and building self-worth and purpose in life can lead to alcohol abuse. And, as I've mentioned before, variation from normal rates of maturation, whether fast or slow, can create challenges for a teen.

## Psychological and Emotional Roadblocks

Some teens experience severe emotional experiences or traumas that block psychological growth. The brain is the center of emotional and behavioral control, as well as reasoning, judgment, and thinking. Anything that blocks a teen's normal emotional and psychological growth or that prevents him from feeling that he fits in or is accepted by others can be discouraging and embarrassing. Typically, these types of problems in teens are traumatic experiences or they persist over long periods of time. If our teen suffers from such problems, professional help may be necessary.

## Social and Economic Disadvantages

Challenges and disadvantages that come from economic and other social circumstances can place families and children in jeopardy of resentment, discouragement, and hopelessness. Self-esteem and opportunities for the development of talents, skills, and interests are often linked to social and economic status. We are making progress at overcoming racial disadvantage, but that and economic and social disadvantages still exist.

Neighborhood and community environments help determine recreation, leisure, and educational opportunities for children. These environments also regulate what is tolerated on the streets, which in turn determines a child's sense of hope, safety, and contribution to the world around him. For example, children who live in communities where little or no productive extracurricular or recreational programs are available, who have little or no financial means to help them-selves, and who live in dangerous, gang-controlled neighborhoods have fewer positive choices. High-risk areas that provide little or no worthwhile social stimuli to children allow for high rates of boredom, gangs, delinquency, and drug abuse. Parents can encourage their teens to recognize and develop special skills, talents, and interests that can provide opportunities. They can work to mobilize their communities and schools to provide safer, better places for their children to grow up. And community and government leaders have the duty to help clean up neighborhoods and to support parents and families in creat-ing meaningful opportunities for their children.

## Learning Disabilities or Challenges

When education is impeded by learning disabilities or other problems, teens come under considerable pressure. When parents and teachers cannot successfully help a teen resolve these problems and find suc-cess, she can become discouraged, hopeless, and rebellious, resulting in problem behavior, which may or may not include drinking. Again, parents can encourage and promote education for their child. They can get their teen into special assistance programs that provide positive methods of learning while de-emphasizing differences. Parental support and encouragement is important.

### Abuse or Neglect

Children who do not receive necessary physical and emotional nurturing and spiritual training, who have their basic needs neglected, or who experience physical, emotional, or sexual abuse are deeply affected by these experiences, often suffering long-term emotional scars that inhibit trust, self-respect, and psychological happiness. Some of these children find that trusting a bottle or a high is safer than trusting a person and that numbing the pain is better than suffering. If our child has suffered abuse, at our hands or the hands of another adult, we have the responsibility to help him work through it and to help him heal. Trauma need not be a lifelong destroyer. Children can recover, but it takes special assistance and loving support from us.

### Alcohol-Induced Pain

Alcohol-induced pain is the emotional turmoil that is directly or indirectly the result of drinking or addiction. Two types of teens fit into the alcohol-induced pain category: the teen who is genetically predisposed to alcoholism and the teen who becomes heavily involved with alcohol for other reasons. Most teenage alcohol abuse stems from curiosity, peer influence, or just wanting to feel good. Problems for teens who are genetically predisposed to alcoholism begin when they take the first drink of alcohol. Up until that point, they may have been well-adjusted kids, fulfilling expectations and responsibilities, and generally free from high-risk emotional or physical problems. This begins to change—sometimes suddenly—when they begin to drink. Not all kids who continue to abuse drugs or alcohol are genetic alcoholics. Heavy, chronic abuse can also lead teens to dependence and addiction.

Whichever way it happens, once a teen is addicted to alcohol, the drug is in control. The alcoholic reacts to the demands of the body to maintain alcohol equilibrium. Drinking now becomes a matter of priority, and craving exercises dominion over love, trust, self-respect, school, sports, interests, hobbies, sober friends, religious groups, values, family, and parents.

These losses, along with isolation and conflict, produce real emotional pain and will stunt a potentially successful life if it continues. Deep within, whether the adolescent recognizes it or not, she begins to form negative feelings and attitudes, such as self-loathing, guilt, shame, remorse, and hopelessness. An addicted teen may begin to see opportunities in life passing her by and feel helpless to control what is happening. She sees relationships, trust, and respect lost with parents and people she has loved. Over time, the feelings become numb so that she no longer loves or trusts anything except the alcohol that feeds her distorted equilibrium.

### How Powerful Are Teen's Emotions?

Most of us can remember how we felt as teens—feeling embarrassed, uncertain, reckless, exuberant, and maybe sometimes powerful. We can remember the pain of rejection, the joy of acceptance, and guilt or shame after doing something stupid or wrong. Sometimes we still feel strong emotions when we think about something that happened to us as teenagers or children. That's how powerful emotions can be.

Unresolved pain is very powerful. Held deep within our core, like hot, molten lava in the earth that is under pressure, unresolved feelings persistently push upward and outward to find expression. This is especially true for teens who do not have thickly developed crusts to hold it in. Even the thickest crusts can someday either explode (in harmful behaviors toward others) or implode (in self-destructive acts), given enough pressure. Teens can be pretty transparent when it comes to strong emotions. They are like active volcanoes, erupting and spewing their feelings all over everyone. They may also go away quietly into drinking, numbing the feelings and avoiding the pain.

Parents, families, teachers, and others may fail to see the symptoms of this inner pain until it erupts in more obvious ways. Sometimes our teen will not recognize or admit it himself. Often our teen does not intend to distress us and deeply regrets his behavior. His actions frequently do not reflect the true emotional pain he's experiencing underneath. When we fail to see deeply the inner pain and act only to treat the symptom behaviors, we are hacking at the leaves instead of striking at the root of the problem.

### The Ring of Attitude

Teen alcoholism is often called a disease of attitudes. By attitudes I mean (1) beliefs that are false or harmful, (2) a negative state of mind, and (3) self-defeating thinking, or what is often called negative self-talk (the silent, critical messages a person sends to herself). They are all connected.

Addiction begins with attitude. It may be as simple as curiosity or innocent experimentation. It may begin with anger or discouragement that is seeking to hurt others or self. Attitude promotes drinking and drinking, in turn, promotes attitude. For example, a teen might be failing at school, perhaps because of a learning problem or because he receives no support at home. He becomes discouraged and begins to believe that he is a failure. He develops an attitude of helplessness and tells himself that he's too dumb or that the teachers are jerks and parents don't care. As a result, he begins skipping school and hanging out with other problem kids. He begins to drink because his newfound friends do and because it makes him feel better. His behavior brings family conflict, arguments, disobedience, trouble in school, or legal problems, increasing stress and further reinforcing his attitude that he is a failure, that all adults are just out to make life miserable, and that the only pleasure in life is drinking with his buddies.

As another example, a teen might be introduced to alcohol at a party. She finds it enjoyable and begins to drink regularly. Drinking brings a sense of guilt because she knows it is unacceptable to her parents and against the law. On the other hand, she thinks that she has a lot of fun and finds drinking enjoyable. She sees herself as a bad person but can't quit drinking. She begins to struggle in school with her grades, loses interest in previously enjoyable activities and positive friendships, and has conflicts with her family. She may even get a reputation with former peers of being a "bad girl." The consequences of her actions reinforce her belief that she is a loser, which further drives her drinking. Eventually, she relinquishes most or even all other values for drinking.

In these examples, we see that drinking can reinforce negative thinking and negative thinking can reinforce drinking. It's called "stinking thinking" in Alcoholics Anonymous circles. As we will learn in chapter 8, this ring of negative attitudes can be intercepted and reversed by stopping the drinking, by learning to reframe the thinking, and by creating a new, more positive experience base. However, if the alcohol abuse is not stopped—if sobriety isn't achieved—the false beliefs and negative attitudes will persist and feed and protect the disease and the painful emotions. It is equally true that if the drinking stops but the negative attitudes or behaviors don't, a teen is at high risk to return to drinking.

### The Ring of Refusal

Alcoholism is a disease of refusals. A common trait of alcoholic teens is their magical and wishful thinking. They continue to believe that they are in control, that they can quit whenever they choose, or that something will change later on and make everything all right. In the later stages of addiction, a teen realizes that he cannot quit because he's tried and failed. He feels fearful, hopeless, and helpless. Yet acceptance of help is as fearful as addiction because it means making changes, learning to trust something other than the bottle, and taking responsibility. Alcoholic teens engage in two significant and dangerous refusals:

1. They refuse to accept responsibility for themselves and their recovery. They make excuses, blame others, deny problems, and lie and deceive others to avoid responsibility or change.
2. They refuse to accept help from other positive people. Sustained by wishful and magical thinking, they refuse or resist help offered by loved ones and professionals around them.

Below are some typical attitudes of refusal from teens who are seriously abusing or are addicted to alcohol.

- I don't care what alcohol does to me. I don't care about anything.
- You can't make me stop using. If I want to use, I'll use.
- I don't need anyone's help. I can do it myself.
- I'm not like the others. I'm not a druggie. I'm doing okay.
- I don't need or want anyone's help. Just leave me alone.
- When I'm ready to stop having fun, I'll stop using. I can do it.

Addicted teens frequently engage in defiance, rejection of advice, avoidance of people and situations that can help, deceit, dishonesty, and theft. If our teen is exhibiting these types of refusal attitudes and behaviors, we should not be turned away or frightened, as frustrating or uncomfortable as they may be. We need to recognize these attitudes as symptoms of a disease. In addiction, dangerous or harmful behaviors cannot be tolerated. We have a right and responsibility to prevent and interdict behaviors that are dangerous or harmful to our child, our family, and others.

### The Ring of Denial

Alcoholism is a disease of denial, and denial can also be a symptom of the coming disease. Alcoholics will deny that their lives are out of control, that they have a disease, and that they are facing serious and life-threatening problems. Denial is a form of numbing—a survival technique essential to many teen alcoholics if they are to survive the discomforts and problems that they experience with addiction.

Denial in addicted teens takes many forms, including masking, secrecy, joking, glamorizing, feeling all-powerful, ignoring, indifference, blaming and fault-finding, anger, rebellion, self-sufficiency, and a false sense of control. Alcoholic teens who engage in alcohol-related delinquency, violence, and socially risky behavior may try to cope with the stressful emotions by denying that problems exist or that their lives are chaotically out of control. Even those who do not engage in this type of behavior, to some degree or another live in an illusion that they are in control of their lives and that they "choose" to use alcohol and engage in certain behaviors because it's fun, exciting, or cool.

Often an addicted teen presents as belligerent, rebellious, cocky, uncaring, or deceitful. This rough outer veneer of behavior and negativism is often, but not always, quite thin in a teen (the adult veneer has had more time to thicken), and beneath the surface are some fairly strong and volatile feelings caused by the heavy price she is paying for addiction and perhaps other challenges in her life. Those teens who suffer from long-term psychological or behavioral problems in addition to alcoholism often have a much thicker crust and are more difficult to work with. The tough-appearing surface of a teen who suffers purely from alcohol addiction (that is, who doesn't suffer from co-occurring psychological problems) cracks pretty quickly when brought into proper treatment, and the teen can make strong gains toward positive growth.

## Loss of Control

It is natural for a teen to want some control in his life. Adolescence is a time for parents to let go of some control—to be counselors rather than decision makers. Just as a chick pecks its way out of a protective eggshell or a caterpillar fights its way out of a cocoon, so a teen struggles to emerge from childhood into an adult world. It is frightening and embarrassing for a teen to admit that control was lost or never gained, especially because of alcoholism or other drug addiction. Parents have the same dilemma in admitting that they have lost control of their teen. Some kids make the mistake of thinking that alcohol helps them have some control. When addicted teens have lost control, it is very improbable that they can regain control by themselves, especially when alcohol has power over them.

## Unwillingness to Make Changes

To an active alcoholic, alcohol is not an evil, enslaving master, and alcohol-free living is not bliss. Alcohol is viewed as a close friend, a buddy that is always there and always provides comfort and cheer. Indeed, when it isn't there, life is filled with discomfort and even pain. Neither is recovery—the achievement of a clean and sober lifestyle—viewed as a liberating blessing but as an undesirable and fearful threat. It would be a grave mistake for parents of an alcoholic teen to view recovery as a walk in the park. It is not easy, but profoundly frightening, challenging, and painful. Alcoholism destroys true trust and love and replaces them with its own. Giving up alcohol leaves an ominous void in the alcoholic's life, as if a close friend or companion died, resulting in grieving.

Once, on a business trip to Hazelden in Center City, Minnesota, I rode on a shuttle with four other adults who were all going to Hazelden's inpatient treatment center for the first time to recover from drug addiction. One was a very nervous, young single woman, perhaps thirty, with addiction to alcohol and diet pills. Another was a housewife in her late twenties, the mother of two children, addicted to pharmacological medications. She had been writing her own prescriptions. Another was a successful, suave musician, in his early thirties, addicted to cocaine since he was fifteen. Last was a man, about forty-five, who had truly bottomed out—he had lost his wife, his children, his job, his health, and nearly his life to drugs. All four of these people had begun abuse in their teens.

For the one-hour ride from the airport to Hazelden, I listened to them tell their stories to each other. That was how they introduced themselves and related to each other: by their drug of choice and drug history. They talked about their use of drugs with great affection and with sadness and discomfort at having to give them up; all but the older man, who was at his rope's end and had been mandated into treatment. Even he, knowing what alcohol and other drugs had done to him, was reluctant to make the change. That was the power of the addiction in their lives. As they stood outside the entrance, nervously taking a last smoke break before they went into the center, I suggested that they look at the entrance as doors to opportunity, rather than to misery.

### What Does Alcoholism Cost?

Alcoholism, like addictions to other drugs, comes with a cost. The severity of this cost depends upon the individual, the circumstances, and the stage of addiction the teen is in. It may permeate most areas of a teen's life or it may be subtle or limited to just one or two areas. It may begin as something fairly benign and unnoticeable, or it may begin with a bang. The one thing that is true about addiction is that eventually the addict will pay a price—and she is not alone. Addiction almost always reaches out to loved ones, friends, and even other people in the community. We can perhaps convince ourselves that we aren't paying a price or that it isn't that bad. We can accept the situation as unavoidable, just part of life. There is always a bottom line with addiction.

The following paragraphs cover some of the "real costs" that families and teens pay for alcohol dependence and addiction. Keeping these in mind is useful because until we recognize the cost, we can't decide if we are willing to pay it. I know people who are house poor and car poor. That is, they drive around in a beautiful luxury car and live in a palace, but they are over their head in debt and don't have time to enjoy any of it because they have to work so hard to pay the bills. They are paying heavily for luxury that eliminates most other pleasures in their lives. I think alcoholism is similar. It can rob our teen and ourselves of many important pleasures in life.

The problems that I have listed below are based on my experiences working with teens and families of addicted teens. Not all addicted or abusing teens pay all of these costs. I know teens I would classify as alcoholic who did not experience many of these problems. It might be a matter of time or situation before a cost is noticeable. Problematic abuse of alcohol also exacts a cost, perhaps not as high as that of addiction but still costly, and the cost continues to rise as long as the abuse of alcohol continues to progress toward addiction.

## The Cost to Education

Most parents have hopes for their children to succeed in school, get an education, and find employment and a fulfilling career. Alcoholic teens may struggle in school because of the effects of drinking or attitude or inability to sustain effort. Some fail or drop out altogether. Parents of an alcoholic teen may endure worries and disappointments as their teen fails tests, doesn't complete or turn in assignments, flunks out of classes, and falls further behind his peers. We may also have to endure the sorrow and embarrassment of dealing with disciplinary measures taken by school administrators, including suspension or even expulsion for misbehavior. Our teen may be drinking on campus, negatively influencing other kids, getting into fights with peers, and behaving belligerently toward teachers and administrators. Our teen may just isolate himself from other people. If our teen is experiencing these types of humiliations, he will be driven deeper and deeper into hopelessness, despair, and angry rebellion.

### The Cost to Family Relationships

Alcohol addiction often disrupts important family relationships. Families are where the most personal and intimate relationships occur, and teens' failure to fulfill their expected role can cause conflict, worry, and pain to everyone. Addicted teens may fail or refuse to perform domestic chores. Their lifestyle changes can be annoying and disconcerting to family members. They may violate and even defy parental rules and treat parents with belligerence and disrespect when confronted. Many families of teenage alcoholics are thrown into chaos and the normal structure and tranquility of the home is lost. Younger children may feel intimidated, even frightened, and disappointed by the conflict and behavior. Addicted teens frequently feel uncomfortable being around the family or disinterested in family events or activities, and want to spend all of their time with peers away from the family. They may even run away from home for extended periods of time, causing parents and other siblings to worry about their whereabouts and health. Frequently, because teens need to have money to purchase alcohol, they steal from parents and siblings, turning the home into a chaos of distrust and forcing family members to live behind lock and key. Sometimes damage is done to the home from drunkenness and conflict.

### The Cost to Social Relationships

Alcoholic teens may lose or let go of positive friendships, even friendships that have existed from childhood, for alcoholic ones. Parents appreciate and depend on their children having positive friendships, and when good kids stop coming around and are replaced with new kids the parents often don't know or suspect to be troublesome, it causes great concern and generates family arguments and conflict. It hurts to see our teen shunned by kids with good standards and goals in life and drifting farther and farther away from the positive, healthful things in life. Depending upon the circumstances, alcoholic teens can become involved in fighting and assaultive behavior with other people. They often drop out of positive youth and church groups. Their reputation can be harmed through a few significant illegal or dishonest incidents, such as stealing from or vandalizing neighbors. Often, because of their behaviors, other family members must endure criticism and embarrassment. Alcoholism is frequently the catalyst and precipitator of sexual activity in a teen's life, being introduced to it through peers and in drinking situations. Sexual activity under the influence of alcohol is dangerous and may result in sexually transmitted disease, unwanted pregnancy, and damage to the teen's ability to form meaningful and healthful relationships with others.

### The Cost to Talents, Interests, and Activities

Alcoholism is a preoccupation that often dominates a teen's life at the expense of important prior interests and activities. An alcoholic teen may lose interest in pursuing talents and interests and activities that once were of great interest and promise. I worked with a boy from Oregon who had been the state's junior amateur golf champion. He gave that up entirely for drugs and alcohol, something he deeply regretted later in treatment. But he decided to take up golf again once he had achieved sobriety and regained a sense of himself, although he was two years older and had missed out on some opportunities. The loss of developing talents, interests, and other positive activities makes a teen shallow and narrow and strips her of her self-esteem, self-confidence, and sense of worth. She may not be able to speak it, but she senses it and is usually filled with a sense of remorse and self-loathing, although she will continue to defend drinking. Of course, parents and other family members are denied the happiness of seeing their loved one excel in something and seeing her find true happiness and success, and this can be disappointing.

### The Cost to Physical and Emotional Health

Chronic alcoholism will sooner or later cause health and emotional problems. Sometimes drinking doesn't have to be chronic to cause problems. Sometimes the problems manifest themselves quickly and unexpectedly, depending upon the teen and the circumstances. This is especially true of emotional problems, because alcoholism frequently causes emotional turmoil in a teen's life. The arguments, the worry, the feelings of guilt, remorse, and bitterness that often come from both parent and child wear on everyone. An addicted teen is going through a series of withdrawals each time he comes off a period of intoxication. Withdrawal may include irritability, paranoia, suspicion, depression, or even thoughts of or attempts at suicide. Our daughter may become pregnant; our son may get a girl pregnant; either may suffer from a sexually transmitted disease. When these situations occur, life isn't fun or interesting anymore, but painful. Of course, there is always the real worry about accident, injury, and death to our own child or someone else's child caused by driving under the influence, overdose, or other thoughtless, intoxicated behaviors. Emotional stress affects our physical health and our sense of happiness and well-being.

### The Cost to Time

Teenage abuse of alcohol is unlawful and, therefore, often fraught with potential legal troubles that can eat up the precious time of youth. The time spent dealing with courts, trials, detention, and treatment add up. Sooner or later, an alcoholic teen who continues to actively drink stands a good chance of winding up arrested, apprehended, or placed in detention for her behavior. It is a progression that I have seen with many teens: it begins as uncontrolled drinking, a ticket for possession, a DUI or two, perhaps a citation for malicious behavior; then stealing, burglary, grand theft auto; a court hearing, detention time, stiff fines, a boot camp or youth work farm; treatment programs, either release time, part-time, or full residential; and possibly hard time in prison. Little by little, step by step, we watch our teen lose her freedom, lose the time of her youth, and lose the opportunities of life, all for the sake of alcohol. It is a heavy price to pay. Some youth manage to avoid much or even all of this cost of lost time; however, they do not avoid all costs. Addiction requires an investment of time and preoccupation with the drug, and the time spent could have been used on more productive activities.

### The Spiritual Cost

Teen alcoholism can be especially hard on spiritual and moral values. The activities and circumstances that alcoholism imposes upon a drinking teen often forces the compromising of personal values, even if it is just a simple disobedience to a standard of behavior expected by parents or society. Often, prior interest in or belief in God or a spiritual Higher Power is lost to addiction. This loss may be partially a by-product of discouragement, hopelessness, and other emotional realities in a teen's life. Physical addictions tend to blur, even blot out, spiritual vision. That is why addiction is typically defined as ending in spiritual bankruptcy—because it devours the scanty spiritual accounts of addicted people, leaving them impoverished and destitute. Faith is lost because trust is completely placed in a substance and little else. Teens typically give up church attendance or membership in youth organizations. They may compromise and relinquish personal, family, and social moral values, deepening their remorse and sense of guilt and shame, but they cannot do anything about it. When alcohol becomes their god, God ceases to exist, and so do parents and families and good friends, for all practical purposes. The addicted teen simply cannot serve two masters, and the addiction always takes precedence. This does not mean that there will not be moments of genuine despair, sorrow, shame, and promises; however, they are generally short-lived and promises are easily broken.

### The Financial Cost

The more tangible costs of alcoholism also place stress on parents, teens, and family members. It might be an eye-opener for families with an addicted teen to add up the estimated tangible and financial costs directly or indirectly caused by alcoholism. I think that such a list would typically include the following: damage to home or property; damage to neighbor's or other public property; personal property (clothing, equipment, household items, etc.) that has been lost or sold for alcohol; property that has been stolen by the teen; money lost from purses, penny banks, credit cards, and bank accounts; fines, tickets, penalties, and other legal court costs; cost of treatment programs or professional help; and money actually expended to pay for alcohol, other drugs, and cigarettes.

It is not to our advantage or even appropriate to keep an exact accounting of the costs of our teens' alcoholism in an effort to hold them accountable for restoring everything they have taken before they can receive our love or acceptance. We love our children above and beyond the material things of this life. Surely they are infinitely more valuable and important than possessions. However, for the sake of breaking through the crust of denial that keeps our emotions insulated and prevents us from exercising helpful action, an exercise of cost accounting is useful. True recovery requires a mending and a forgiving, and this healing demands some type of a recognition, accounting, and penitence before the mercy of the love that we have for each other can bring about the miracle of forgiveness. It simply does not work to sweep all the pain and suffering under the rug of denial.

### The Ring of Addiction

The outer ring of crust in our addiction model—the part that we see manifested in our teen's appearance, language, relationships, and behaviors—is the actual addiction playing itself out in daily life. Teenage addiction shows itself in many different forms, but typically we see some fairly common traits. Those traits were explained in chapter 4.

An example of the addiction process is seen in John's life. John is fifteen years old. As a child, he seemed active and fairly normal, was bright and creative. As John grew and began to explore outside the home, he began to manifest some social and behavioral problems. John had particular trouble focusing in school and completing his work. He was clearly bright enough to do the work and excelled in art class, but he would not complete his assignments or turn them in. He couldn't find them half the time, and he always seemed off task. John had difficulty relating to friends, especially as he moved into puberty. He didn't seem to know how to read other kids and relate to their needs.

In his unassuming way, he seemed almost oblivious to others as he impulsively acted out. Eventually, John drove away most of his friends, which created great emotional pain for him, but he didn't seem to be able to follow the coaching of his parents or others who tried to help. His teachers were frustrated, and his parents figured it was just a stage that John was going through. But by the time he moved into middle school, the problems had worsened. He wandered about the classroom, fidgeted, and bothered other students. His clever wit and classroom antics to get attention further alienated him from his classmates. His social relationships suffered, and he was disliked, made fun of, and ignored by his peers.

John's parents put a lot of pressure on him to shape up and do better, but nothing seemed to motivate him. His self-esteem was shattered by his teachers' criticism and his classmates' rejection. Eventually, he just gave up. He became disinterested in school and began to spend more time by himself.

One day, John discovered alcohol through a friend in the neighborhood named Joey. Joey's older brother could get him alcohol anytime he wanted it. At first, John was reluctant to drink because he thought it would get him into trouble, but he discovered that the alcohol made him feel good and took away the pain. He and Joey began hanging out with Joey's older brother and his friends, and soon, John felt accepted into a brotherhood. He had a new, important image among his schoolmates. John knew that he would be in trouble if his parents found out that he was drinking alcohol, but the emotional anesthesia that came from drinking was more powerful than any fear he had of being caught. Soon John was spending much of his time with his new friends, drinking alcohol and getting drunk. His schoolwork suffered even more, and he began to skip school to hang out with his friends and drink.

John's lifestyle began to change. He didn't seem to care about his appearance or grooming, as he had in the past. His language and deportment became coarse and aggressive. His early interests in art and swimming were abandoned. Kids who used to try to tolerate and befriend him disappeared and were replaced by boys of another peer group—older boys who often smelled of tobacco. John was gone from home most of the time. He resisted telling his parents where he went, what he was doing, and with whom he spent his time, but they had suspicions. He didn't eat meals with the family, and when he was at home, he was argumentative and disrespectful. He sneaked out of the home and stayed out late at night and often had problems getting up for school in the morning. He refused to do any chores around the home or to keep his room clean. His parents noticed that when he was home, he picked on his younger siblings or spent all of his time isolated in his room, listening to music. He was moody, emotionally volatile, and defensive.

John began to steal from his family, breaking into his siblings' piggy banks, stealing money from his mother's purse and father's wallet, and even using their debit card to withdraw money from their account. John's parents were forced to put locks on their bedroom doors and those of their children to prevent John from stealing. He denied any wrongdoing when members of his family complained or questioned him about the missing money. Often he became angry and belligerent and threatened to beat them up or do other harm to them if they didn't back off.

John's parents and school principal confronted him after his teachers made several reports of truancy and school failure, but he belligerently said he did not like school and that he did not care whether he failed. He was put on probation by the school and grounded by his parents, but he defied the sanctions and eventually ran away for several days. When he returned, he was gaunt, disheveled, and tired from a three-day drunken binge. He slept for two days. When he did come out of his room, he was fidgety, sweaty, nauseated, and emotionally volatile. Still in denial, he refused to take any responsibility for his actions and blamed his parents and family and school principal. Within a few more weeks, his parents had lost complete control. John was expelled from school for the remainder of the year. He was soon arrested by police, along with other boys, and charged with possession and use of alcohol and criminal mischief and trespassing. The judge mandated John to complete a residential treatment program. In the treatment program, John was diagnosed with attention deficit disorder (ADD) and substance addiction to alcohol.

John's parents were shocked to hear this diagnosis. They were baffled by what had happened to him, changing from a bright, enthusiastic boy into a deviant, rebellious alcoholic in less than a year. They hadn't seen it coming, hadn't recognized the learning problems that had made school and socializing such a miserable failure, and hadn't realized that his circumstances and environment had led him into becoming an alcoholic.

There are other illustrations that we could describe: (1) the economically and socially advantaged child who seems to have all the benefits that family, race, and money can provide, who becomes involved in alcohol, perhaps first in high school and then later, as a binge drinker in a college fraternity; (2) the child from an abusive and addicted home, whose life has been filled with pain and a void of supportive relationships and who seeks alcohol to cope with life; (3) the teen from a single-parent home where the mother works and is going to school to gain a better-paying job and who lives in a neighborhood filled with boredom, gangs, drugs, and violence because that's all they can afford; (4) the seemingly well-adjusted youth who is succeeding in school and extracurricular activities and has good friends and a supportive family, who experiments with alcohol and plummets into alcoholism; (5) the victim of sexual, emotional, and physical abuse who uses alcohol to cope with the pain and becomes a prostitute for sex to provide for her alcoholism and to act out her self-loathing and need to harm herself.

These are just a sampling from legions of lives. They speak loudly and clearly that alcoholism, on its own and in combination with unresolved trauma, discouragement, and other painful emotions, can and does ruin young lives and the lives of parents and family.

## Mirrors to the Soul

We cannot see deeply into other people, even our own teens. We may think that we know our children, but we can see only what they let us see, what they tell us about, and often these are but fleeting images reflected on the mirror surface of their lives. This is especially true in our busy world where both parents are working to pay the bills or a single parent is raising a family. We pause, periodically and momentarily, to check in with each other; we make relatively quick janitorial checks; but we often fail to maintain deep connections. For this reason, we cannot judge each other's worth based on what we see. And those folk who are placed in positions where they must judge on behalf of schools and communities must be diligent to look beyond outer behavior and to look more deeply into the soul.

Parents, siblings, and others are often baffled and upset by the disruptive behavior of a teen who has become so uncharacteristic of his former self. They often do not see the hidden roots of the problems and the denial, refusal, pain, and deep-seated false beliefs and negative attitudes that surround the emotionally distressed alcoholic teen.

In summary, it remains to be said that the value of our addiction model, with its defensive rings, lies in its ability to help parents and others see the deeper problems that lie below the waterline in an addicted teen's life. These addicted and seriously abusing kids are not simply inert blocks of ice floating chaotically about on the surface of life but are troubled and distressed human beings. Their emotions and defenses rip holes in the lives of those who live closest to them or who attempt to get close enough to help. The model of addiction helps provide mirrors into the deeper souls of troubled teens, enabling parents to be more proactive.

I encourage parents who read this book to take more quality and quantity time with their children. Let us shore up our homes and make them places where children are taught healthy values and a strong work ethic. Let us set our standards firm and rally our children around us in love. Let us talk with our children about our concerns, opinions, and desires. Let us limit and discipline our children with kindness and sincerity. Let us lead from the front by example and not just precept. I invite families to spend time together on a regular basis in family councils—to have fun, learn something, strengthen values and bonds of love, and coordinate schedules. Meals are helpful times for this. We need to make family and children a priority.

# Chapter 6

# Reasons to Save:
# Can We Really Make a Difference?

Years ago, when I was a young Marine lieutenant, a platoon commander, I took my hard chargers to requalify in water survival. Marines are soldiers of the sea and must be able to survive in water. Each Marine was to jump off a fifteen-foot tower, fully clothed in boots and fatigues and helmet. After demonstrating the correct entry method, each Marine was to surface and remain afloat in the pool for a period of time.

One young man, a black Marine at a time when racial conflict was high, froze on the tower. I coaxed and encouraged him, but he would not jump. Eventually, he told me that he was not a strong swimmer and that, clothed and helmeted, he was fearful that he would not be able to stay afloat.

As a young, brash Marine, who had been a lifeguard in college, I pulled the shepherd's crook, a long pole with a hook on the end, from its place and told him that if he would jump, I would extend the shepherd's crook to him. All he had to do was grasp it, and I would pull him up.

I don't remember being surprised at his response at that particular moment because I was used to men obeying orders, but now, as one who more fully appreciates the principles of trust in behavior, I am flabbergasted by what happened. Almost without hesitation, the

Marine shouted, "Sir, yes sir!" and jumped. His expectations proved to be prophetic. He went straight to the bottom and stood there with his arms outstretched, tiny air bubbles coming from between pursed lips, waiting for the touch of the shepherd's crook. I extended the pole, he grasped it, and I pulled him to the surface.

Similarly, each teen jumps into life and struggles to stay afloat. Some have it easier than others. Some of us know what it is like to sink to the bottom of life and feel the pain and fear that comes with knowing that we cannot make it to the top without help. How remarkable it is when someone extends the shepherd's crook to us and lifts us up.

Extending and grasping are action words. We cannot save our teen from addiction unless she is willing to be saved, unless she is willing to grasp hold of the shepherd's crook that we extend to her. And our teen cannot save herself without help from us. In this regard, I use the term *save* to mean doing our part in helping her to recover, to learn to live a fulfilling life without alcohol or other drugs. In reality, saving means helping someone else save herself.

There are compelling reasons to help save a teen who is drowning in alcoholism, and there are compelling reasons for an addicted teen to recover. Four compelling reasons to save and be saved are important to keep in mind, because it is certain that the teen, embroiled in alcohol dependence, will not see the need for or have the hope of recovery. Parents, too, can lose vision and hope.

## The Human Soul Is Worth Saving

If we are the parents of an alcoholic teen, we may have reached a breaking point where we seriously question whether we can go on with the nightmare lifestyle we have been living. We may be angry that the family is sacrificing life and happiness. We may wonder where this angry, frightening person, once an innocent little boy or girl, came from. Giving up hope on a child is a soul-wrenching experience. If we are at a point where trust and respect have been dashed to pieces, we need to remember without a doubt that our teen is worth saving, no matter how troubled he may be. Deep down our child is uniquely wonderful and inherently good. Each human soul is worth saving, and there are positive steps that can be taken to help. What is needed is *vision, knowledge of the disease, effective action,* and *support* through family and community-based resources.

More often than not, a teen who is addicted doesn't think he is worth saving. Whether he admits it or not, he's lost faith and hope. He probably doesn't believe that he can be saved, nor is he willing to put forward the effort to save himself. Misery is, after all, familiar and therefore comforting. He's discouraged, guilt-ridden, ashamed, and frightened, so much so that the thought of losing his only comfort—alcohol—is unbearable. He's tried at times to quit drinking, only to fail. He has hurt himself and others whom he loves or from whom he wants respect so many times that he believes himself to be a failure and a waste, unable and perhaps unworthy of recovery. A clean and sober lifestyle seems a rapidly fading dream, sometimes even faded to the point of oblivion.

Alcoholism inspires dependence, and dependence requires the sacrifice of individuality and self-respect. A teen will sacrifice all in her life that inspires self-worth and self-confidence for alcohol. For a teen to recover, she must first see her worth, which is more often than not masked behind layers of self-loathing and negative feelings. Before a teen can see her own worth, parents must see it first.

### Life Has an Important Purpose

Perhaps one of the greatest tragedies in life is the person who never discovers his special purpose and never rises to his potential. If there is no purpose in life, there is no purpose in saving or recovering. We might as well die on the bottom of the pool as up on the bank. Some people find great purpose for their lives, and others find none. I believe that life has a grand purpose for everyone regardless of circumstance or walk of life, and I believe that every person, adult and teen, has the opportunity and responsibility to discover what that purpose is.

Recovery from alcoholism or other drug addiction requires a discovery of purpose. Without purpose there is no reason, no vision, no motivation. But discovery of purpose is a personal thing. It is not so much that a parent dictates a child's purpose in life, but a wise parent will help the child discover it for himself, and when he discovers purpose, it will serve as a lighthouse to keep him on the path and bring him safely home.

The nineteenth-century naturalist and philosopher Henry David Thoreau wrote in his notes on Walden Pond: "Youth gets together its materials to build a palace or, perchance, a bridge to the moon, but, alas, at length the middle-aged man concludes to build a woodshed with them." A teen will become whatever she values. What she values she will do. What she persists in doing, she will become. The teen who seeks only pleasure, excitement, fun, control, acceptance, or feeding an addiction neglects the inner, deeper improvements of character. The teen caught in the trap of alcoholism is inspired only by craving and obsessing and will not prosper. Middle-aged woodsheds begin in youth and are filled with illusions, pain, and hopelessness. Alcoholism creates woodsheds.

Bob Richards, the great onetime Olympic gold medalist, during a speech gave this secret of what makes an Olympian: "Human life needs an inner response, a susceptibility to greatness, which is desire." If a teen's life is a woodshed, purpose will be lost on him. He will simply not see it. It will not inspire him to recover or become a better person. Parents and other responsible adults have the privilege to inspire purpose and desire.

## We Have the Power to Become What We Will

In *The Wizard of Oz*, when Dorothy was about to leave her friends in Oz and return home to Kansas, the good witch told Dorothy that she had always possessed the power to return home. All she had to do was click the heels of her magical red shoes together three times and repeat the words "There's no place like home." This amazed Dorothy, for she had always seen herself as powerless and dependent upon the great and powerful Oz to regain her home in Kansas. In fact, all of the other main characters—the lion who wanted courage, the tin man who wanted a heart, and the scarecrow who wanted a brain—already had them; they just had to discover them.

So it is with recovery, with other important accomplishments in life. Our teen has the power to recover from alcoholism and to regain a happy, productive life. She just has to realize this and see beyond self-imposed limitations. I do not mean to say that this is as easy as clicking heels together. It can be very challenging, but very worth it, and the only way to true recovery is along the yellow brick road of self-empowerment.

Father Maple, in Herman Melville's classic novel *Moby Dick*, teaches us something about this self-empowerment. Says he: "All things that God would have us do are hard, and hence, he oftener commands us than endeavors to persuade. And if we obey God, we must disobey ourselves, and it is in this disobeying of ourselves wherein the hardness of obeying God consists."

I find this statement helpful as a parent and grandparent because it reminds me that my family and I have the responsibility as well as the power to act. We have the power to disobey our nature and desires—our ego—when harmful and to obey something higher, better, and more powerful than ourselves. It reminds me of my dependence upon a Higher Power and its essential nature in recovering from addiction.

It is a truth that recovery from addiction requires a certain disobeying of ourselves and our addictive nature. It requires a changing of beliefs, attitudes, thoughts, feelings, behaviors, and relationships that are destructive, self-defeating, or enabling to continued addiction. It is not easy to disobey oneself or the voice of addiction, but lasting recovery is significantly enhanced when we surrender our own nature to a Higher Power and to a pathway that leads upward. Nothing in my life has been more powerful in helping me successfully overcome difficult challenges than my faith in myself and in God.

In the end, the only way to save a teen, or any other person for that matter, is to help her save herself. The power must come from within and without. The truth is, we can't save a child who refuses to be saved. We can postpone self-destruction, maybe, but we can't force her to recover. She will save herself only if she has a vision and desire to do so. Vision inspires purpose, purpose inspires effort, and effort produces outcomes. "Every action we take, everything we do," said Anne Burkhe, a counselor, "is either a victory or a defeat in the struggle to become what we want to become."

### Becoming Real through Real Principles

Real things are governed by real principles. The world we live in is governed by real laws: physical, spiritual, and civil. We can discover and follow these real principles, which will lead us to things that are real, such as happiness, peace, success, and self-worth.

I grew up in farm country, living close to nature and watching the cycle of seasons go around each year. We planted in the spring, we cultivated and watered in the summer, we harvested in the autumn, and we slept in the winter. The physical laws that govern the harvest of nature also govern the harvesting of human souls. Wise are the parents and teens who understand and follow these laws, instead of selectively ignoring them or trying to become a law unto themselves.

### The First Law: We Reap What We Sow

It is a truism that seeds bring forth like fruit. Apple seeds produce apples, not potatoes. If we plant weeds, we harvest weeds. If we plant sorrow, we reap sorrow. There are seeds that, if planted and cultivated, will grow into alcohol abuse and addiction. Several of those seeds have been discussed in earlier chapters. A child seldom plants with the end in mind. Sometimes parents are equally guilty. We sometimes sow thoughtlessly, only to discover when it is time to harvest that we have weeds, and we rush about to try to turn weeds into marketable produce.

If we, as parents, want to know what attitudes and beliefs and behaviors to cultivate, we need to first consider the harvest. Begin with the end in mind, as Stephen Covey teaches in his organizational management conferences. We can ask ourselves: *What do I want to enjoy when the season of harvest is come? What do I want my child to enjoy?* Then plant accordingly. There are no bad human seeds; only bad soil, harsh environments, and neglectful sowers.

### The Second Law: We Reap More Than We Sow

Out of little things come great things, both good and bad. From one apple seed comes an entire orchard of apple trees. From one small, seemingly inconsequential act can come years of happiness or misery. One drink today can result in a lifetime of pain and misery. From one false belief can come a lifetime of lost opportunity.

### The Third Law: We Reap in a Different Season Than We Sow

The things children do and the habits they form today will bear fruit tomorrow. Teenage drinking that is tolerated today may be condemned and punished tomorrow. A drinking teenager may be winked at by society as engaging in normal experimentation and merely having normal teenage fun. As an adult alcoholic who cannot keep a job, a marriage, or a family or who is a criminal, abuser, or social burden, he will be judged and punished by society. When did the seed of alcoholism get planted? Usually as a teen.

### The Fourth Law: We Cannot Change Our Present Harvest, but We Can Plant Anew

Some seeds we planted and cultivated on our own; others we had no control over. For example, a child has no control over inheriting the addictive gene, but she does have control over whether she drinks or uses drugs. She does have control over whether she recovers. It is important for parents and responsible adults to help teens take responsibility for the things in life that they have power to affect and responsibility to control, such as their own feelings and conduct, and not for those things over which they have no control.

An alcoholic teen, having made serious mistakes, believes that he has committed the unpardonable sin and that there is no hope for penitence or forgiveness. He needs to know that life is not one season of growth and harvest but many microseasons. Each new hour, each new day, each week, month, and year is a new season of opportunity. Each new decision in life is a chance to plant anew. Neither parents nor children need lie seedlike and helpless, for the power is in them to plant and to determine their own harvest, and there are compelling reasons to do so.

# Prevention and Diversion: Can Alcoholism Be Prevented?

$A$lcoholism is preventable. The best way to prevent it is not to use alcohol or other drugs of abuse. We cannot prevent our child from inheriting the addiction gene if it runs in the family, but we can follow measures that will help prevent abuse and addiction. Anything we can do to *delay* alcohol use is to our advantage. Statistics show that if drinking is delayed until age twenty-one, a child's risk of serious alcohol problems decreases by 70 percent.[1] As we noted earlier, children who begin drinking in their early teens have a significant chance of having alcohol problems throughout their lives. So it's worth doing all we can to prevent teenage drinking or to at least postpone the age that a child takes his first drink.

### Prevention Requires Teamwork
Prevention becomes most effective when the same message about alcohol abuse and alcoholism is delivered by multiple messengers in a teen's life—schools, parents, peers, and the community. The trick is to get everyone singing from the same sheet of music and in harmony. The message must be consistent and must not be sent only once but continually throughout the teen years, and all members of the team need to send the same message. Mixed messages only weaken a child's understanding and resolve. We cannot directly control the messages

135

others send about alcohol, but we can set the standard and the environment in our own lives and in our home. We can limit and counter any media messages that come into our home. We can coach our teen and provide her with a kind of mental armor as she goes to school and socializes with friends by caringly and respectfully teaching values and standards and expectations. We can look for the chinks in her armor and help strengthen those areas. We can promote awareness and positive action among neighbors and within our schools and communities.

### How Do I Talk to My Teen?

Talking with our teen about our feelings about alcohol and other drug abuse is important. We may fear that bringing up the subject of alcohol abuse with our teen will serve only to pique his curiosity and steer him toward it instead of away from it. But silence from us on the subject only increases the risk. Our child needs to know what we think and feel about alcohol. He needs to know what is important to us. Better that he learn about alcohol from us than from a peer or someone who does not fully understand our values. Better that our child be prepared to respond to the challenge or invitation when we aren't around than to try to wing it on his own. If we don't set the standard regarding the use of alcohol, then someone else will, and it may not be an acceptable standard. One key thing I've learned as a parent is that my children picked up and internalized much more of what I tried to teach them than I thought they had. When I thought they were simply brushing me off or bored out of their minds, they were listening. They just didn't want to appear that they were, and they needed time to mull things over and come to their own conclusions.

### Communicating without Intruding

We need to remember that we are talking to teenagers, not small children. Teens desperately want to make their own decisions and resist undue intrusion. We can treat them the way our friends would want to be treated. Making "I" statements instead of "you" statements is a helpful method of speaking. "You" statements lay blame and convey criticism and suspicion. "I" statements simply describe how we feel, what we see, and what we want and are far less likely to inspire resentment or cause teens to feel that we are intruding upon their need to make their own decisions.

### I Care

The old adage is always true: "What you do speaks so loudly that I can't hear what you say." Our child's desire to listen to us will be greatly influenced by how much she thinks we care, and that will be decided by our actions more than by our words. Make it clear that the reason we want to talk with her is that we care about her and about the things she does. Let her know that drinking alcohol is a big issue and that it matters to us; we care about her because we love her; we care about drinking because it is illegal, dangerous, and possibly against our family's values; we care enough to warn and forewarn her about alcohol: "I love you very much, and I don't want anything bad to happen to you."

### I See

We explain to our teen what we have seen that prompts us to want to talk to him about alcohol use. This is the time to share with him important information about drinking and to share our point of view. We need to be accurate and honest, and not sugarcoat what we have to say, beat around the bush, or try to scare him, and we need to avoid unfair speculation and preaching. For example: "I've noticed that you have beer posters on your wall . . . that you have new friends . . . that you're going to parties where I think alcohol is served. I'd like to talk with you about that."

*I Feel*

After telling our child what we have seen, we can explain to her how we feel about it and why. This provides the impetus, the feeling, the power behind the information. As this is the emotional part of our message, we need to make sure we've got control of our emotions. We don't want to act out of anger or worry, as this is only self-serving and is harmful to the communication. Being honest is the best approach. "I have strong feelings about alcohol. I am strongly opposed to you, or any member of our family, drinking alcohol or being with people who are drinking."

Parents who drink moderately should honestly tell their children this and not be afraid to explain their recognition of its potential danger. They shouldn't be shy about establishing the legal differences between them and their child and explaining the greater dangers for teenage use. For example: "I choose to have an occasional drink of wine [or other beverage], but I never let it get out of control or become dangerous to me or others. When you are of legal age to drink, you may make that decision for yourself. But until then, I do not want you to drink, and I need to be able to trust you on this because it is very important to me."

A parent who has a spouse, a former spouse, a parent, or other relative who is an alcoholic needs to remember that his or her teen has also experienced this situation, sometimes very intimately, and is forming his own opinions about alcohol. Sensitivity to his experience and an openness about the circumstances and dangers of alcohol abuse need to be clearly communicated. It does little good to condemn the alcoholic, but more good to explain the powers of alcohol upon otherwise good people. When alcoholism is evident in generations of a family, warnings to the child of the potential of a genetic inheritance and predisposition to alcoholism can be important to communicate. For example: "You and I both know from our own experiences what out-of-control alcohol abuse can do to a person and a family. Your father wasn't always the way you see him now as an alcoholic. He was once a wonderful, caring man, and in some ways he still is when he's not under the influence. But he can no longer control his drinking, and it's destroying him and our relationship with him. I don't want you to suffer the same thing as your father. Children of parents who are alcoholics are at high risk to become alcoholic if they start to drink. For these reasons, it is very important that you promise me and keep the promise that you will not use alcohol, at least until you are twenty-one years of age. If you are tempted to use, come to me and talk with me about it first, and I will help you."

Parents who are in recovery from alcoholism can benefit their children by talking honestly and directly about their insights from the experience and the pitfalls in attitudes, beliefs, thoughts, and feelings that led them into alcoholism. Hiding the truth because of embarrassment, shame, or pride is self-serving and does not help our children. It is important that we do not exaggerate our perceptions either positively or negatively but speak frankly and openly. We can help our teens compare our experience to their own, using it as a teaching tool.

### I Want

We can tell our children clearly what we want or need them to do. Children need to know what course of action their parents want them to take. Remove the guesswork and the need for interpretation. It will strengthen our children in times of temptation or pressure when we are not there to help them. For example: "I cannot accept or allow you to drink alcohol, at least not until you are of legal age. I want to know that I can trust you when you are gone from the home to make good decisions and to obey the laws and our rules. I want you to promise me that you will not drink or go places with people who do drink."

It is equally important that we listen to our children. They see and feel and want also. Effective communication is both listening and speaking openly and honestly. Fail to do either and we fail to communicate. Failed diplomacy always results in armed conflict if the issue is important enough to either side.

### *I Will*
We can tell our child what we will do to help or support her and the consequences that must come if our wishes are not followed. We need to set clear limits and expectations and to provide fair consequences, always established and presented in the spirit of love and compassion, but with clarity and resolve. This helps our teen realize that we are serious about preventing the problem and that she needs to get serious. It also provides valuable support and structure for the future. Some teens aren't strong enough to stand up for themselves in front of peer pressure. To be able to draw upon the parents' power by saying that Mom and Dad would kill her if they found out about her drinking is better than nothing. Hopefully, she will develop a backbone at some point and stand on her own. If we have failed to set limits or to provide discipline for misbehavior in the past, our teen will resent and resist our efforts. She may fight limits and consequences, but down deep she wants and needs them. Fences and discipline reinforce her sense of worth.

### Reducing Risk and Increasing Protection
Prevention works best when parents pay attention to some key risk and protective factors. Many of these risk and protective factors can help us predict possible problems of alcohol use in our teen. Reducing risk factors and promoting protective factors reduces the likelihood that our teen will use alcohol or other drugs. Reducing just one of these risk factors in a teen's life may reduce other factors at the same time. Increasing just one protective factor may help our

child develop a healthier lifestyle and resist the influence to use.

## Risk Factors

Below are some factors that can increase the risk of a teen using alcohol.

- Chaotic home environment (argument; lack of structure, routine, rules, discipline)
- Ineffective parenting (lack of or inconsistent time together, discipline, limit setting, supervision)
- Little mutual attachment and nurturing
- Inappropriate, shy, or aggressive child behavior in social settings (including the classroom)
- Academic failure
- Low academic aspirations
- Poor social coping skills (making and keeping friends, sharing skills, communication skills)
- Friendships and associations with deviant peers
- Negative neighborhood and community environments
- Perceived approval of drug use by parents, family, community
- Parental substance abuse or mental illness

Parents should review these and other risk areas and establish specific ways to minimize, reduce, or eliminate them. We are not helpless, and there are many support programs and organizations available. However, positive action begins at home with parents and families.

## Protective Factors

Protective factors are things that help shield or protect teens from the potential risk of alcohol abuse and addiction. These include the natural strengths, values, and competencies that our children possess and those found within our family, neighborhood, schools, and community support networks. We can look closely at our children, our family, and the community system that they are growing up in and work to enhance the protective factors for their benefit. It might be helpful for us as parents to review and check those factors that are operative for us and our children.

- Strong family bonds (healthy, active, positive relationships)
- Parental engagement in the child's life (monitoring, coaching, intervening)
- Clear parental expectations and consequences
- Academic success (positive academic environment/structure)
- Strong bonds with schools, communities, and churches (activities and support)
- Norms, beliefs, and values that support abstinence
- Protective, healthy community environments
- Positive activities and developmental youth programs

### Prevention Strategies

National, state, and community organizations are focusing greater efforts on preventing or diverting alcohol abuse and alcoholism among teenagers. Being aware of what is being done in our state, city, and community will help us make appropriate use of those techniques and programs.

As stated earlier, effective prevention requires that several or all major institutions within a society give the same message consistently to a teen about alcoholism and drinking. The family is the core of our social institutions, and parents are the heart and core of the family. Social institutions and government organizations cannot look at the family and say, we have no need of you, and vice versa. When it comes to teens, everyone is important and everyone must work together, or else the effort is weakened, with cracks and pockets into which teens will inevitably fall.

As parents, we have the responsibility and opportunity to develop appropriate prevention strategies within our family. As members of the community, school district, city, state, and nation, we also have a right to participate in the development of meaningful programs and strategies that will bless the lives of families.

Some meaningful guidelines for prevention of underage drinking have been recommended by researchers and the National Coalition of Governors' Spouses.[2]

## Family Strategies

The family is the heart and soul of prevention efforts. Time and again research shows that when a family is positively involved in a teen's life, the teen is better off than those without positive family support. We needn't doubt our own purpose and value, because we have several important tasks to take on as a family in order to prevent problems.

### Education and Skills Training

We can become educated on alcohol and teen issues that may place our teens at risk. While we cannot directly control our children's decisions about alcohol use, we can educate them with current, accurate information about alcohol. We can also educate ourselves, as parents, about the issues so that we can maneuver through the minefields of false information and beliefs that surround our children.

Alcoholism is not just a family member abusing alcohol. Its prevention and cure is connected with communication and parenting skills in the family. All parents can learn to communicate more effectively with their children. To discipline undesirable behavior, for example, they can use natural and logical consequences that build responsibility instead of merely empowering parents. They can seek to better understand their children and to listen to them. They can strengthen family interaction. Help can be obtained from books, family counselors, and community and special classes.

## Safe Home Environment

Parents and children can decide what kind of an environment they want in their home. Home is the sovereign world of a family. Nothing need come into it or influence it without agreement. It works best when parents and children decide together and agree on a standard of living and on values by which to live. Many families are deciding to make a family pledge to maintain a safe home environment that is alcohol-free. Family pledges generally contain at least the following commitments:

1. To provide adult supervision for all children visiting the home
2. To reduce or eliminate the availability of alcohol in the home
3. To provide secure storage areas for all alcohol in the home
4. Not to allow parties or gatherings at home when parents are absent
5. Not to allow children to drink alcohol in the home
6. To talk with and cover for other parents with similar commitments

## Communication

We can make discussing alcohol and other drugs with our children a priority. We need to talk to them regularly about many things, not just alcohol, and do it at a time when they are most receptive. We need to ask them about their friends, their activities, their school, and other events. If other children in the neighborhood or community are drinking, we can find out how our child feels about it, what concerns he has, and any pressures he may be under. We can express feelings and give counsel. Our child needs to fully understand the laws governing alcohol use and the consequences of being caught with alcohol, both from a legal standpoint and a parental standpoint.

If we use alcohol—even if we have problem use—or if we have used in the past, we can talk openly and frankly with our children about the reasons we use and why we do not want them to use, explaining the pitfalls or dangers that we see in using alcohol, without resorting to threats or using scare or control tactics. Such tactics don't work and will only harm our credibility. We can listen and talk to our kids as people we love and respect and for whom we have a responsibility. We can invite their questions and opinions, not as threats but as opportunities to communicate. If we drink and have never experienced negative consequences from drinking, we need to be careful that we do not hold that up as absolute proof that alcohol is not potentially dangerous and that it's okay for children to use. We need to alert them to the potential dangers of drinking and to measures we have taken to avoid them, reaffirming the request that they not drink while underage.

### Monitoring

Monitoring children takes an investment of time and self. Perhaps we have built in too many surrogate baby-sitters (television, electronic games, Internet, etc.) in our society. We may need to disengage a little from all the other things that occupy our time and mind and observe our children more closely, being aware of their moods, appearance, language, activities, and friendships and asking them about their opinions. This helps teens develop their values and opinions, and it helps parents stay tuned to their children's attitudes. Being aware of emerging signals of distress and destructive patterns can help us head off later problems.

## Staying Involved

We need to be as involved in our child's life and extracurricular activities as possible—taking the time to show interest in her activities, knowing what she is doing, and attending key events when appropriate (or ensuring that she is properly chaperoned). I remember watching a young father, obviously busy with earning a living, at his young daughter's soccer game. He had made the effort to be physically present at the game, but he spent most of his time standing behind the bleachers talking business on his cell phone. Being not only physically but emotionally present at important events in our child's life sends an affirming message. We shouldn't push the training and disciplining and raising of our child solely onto others. We need to be involved in community issues and organizations that affect children and family.

## Setting Clear Expectations and Discipline

Our child will be less likely to engage in problem drinking if he feels close to us and if he knows we care. A clear signal is sent to our child when we set clear expectations and limits regarding drinking alcohol and associating with people who drink; that signal is that he is important and precious to us. When expectations and limits are followed up with fair and consistent discipline, we measurably increase our child's potential to avoid drinking.

## Promoting Self-Discipline

We do not want our children to be dependent on our limits and controls all their lives. We want them to become self-governing and to have intelligent and healthy attitudes. Self-discipline requires loyalty to principles and values, and it requires self-confidence, or what is often called positive psychological autonomy. This simply means that through our teaching and disciplining and handling, we promote self-confidence, self-worth, and a belief in our children that they can trust their own values and decisions.

## Extracurricular Activities

Approximately 40 percent of our child's day is discretionary time, which presents enormous potential for negative, or unhealthy, activities. It is known that youth without adult supervision or structure are significantly more likely to drink. A high percentage of first-time experimentation and early abuse comes as a result of child boredom and lack of supervision. Children need to have positive fun and leisure recreation. They learn important skills through extracurricular activities.

### Alternative Programs

Researchers have found that programs that offer activities for kids that are more appealing than boredom and drinking alcohol can be effectively run in communities. School, community, and church youth groups and recreation programs can provide activities such as athletic events, sporting events, service projects, fine arts activities, and others that are of interest to teens. Alternative programs tend to fill time and provide healthy activity, but they are not as effective as programs that teach useful life skills.

### Peer Programs

Peer programs have been found to be even more effective than alternative programs. Peer programs bring teens together in interesting activities that also provide training in important life skills, refusal skills, and assertiveness and have been shown to significantly reduce underage drinking. Results in the communities where these types of programs are run show marked improvement in life skills, communication skills, psychological stability, school performance, and neighborhood safety and a drop in risky behavior and juvenile delinquency.

## Social Strategies

A strong relationship has been found to exist between alcohol use in youth and social, emotional, and behavioral problems. Here are some actions that parents can take to directly or indirectly influence teens:

- Work to reduce or eliminate conflict, argument, or violence in the home.
- Encourage and promote positive friendships for children.
- Promote involvement in positive community or church youth groups.
- Keep communication lines open.
- Discuss and resolve important emotional stressors or problems teens may have.
- Stay attuned to children's academic performance and progress.
- Regulate the type of literature, music, and television that comes into the home.
- Support or help organize social and public health programs that benefit teens.
- Help children maintain a healthy lifestyle: physical, social, emotional, and spiritual.
- Support law enforcement and legal institutions in enforcing drinking laws.
- Don't allow children to attend underage drinking parties.

## School Strategies

School programs can be more effective when they are supported by families, peers, and the community. Parents can assist school leaders and teachers in establishing healthful policies for their children by getting involved in Parent-Teacher Associations (PTA) and other forums. Studies have proved that when families, schools, community leaders, and proprietors form a coalition, underage drinking can be minimized. Good school policies promote values, statutes, and methods that define expected performance and behavior standards of students, teachers, and administration within the school environment. The Governor's Coalition named the following elements of good policy (see www.alcoholfreechildren.org/gs/pubs/html/prev.htm):

- Prohibition of alcohol and alcohol use on school grounds or school facilities, at school-sponsored activities, and while students are representing the school
- Clear consequences for violating the policy
- Assessing and referring students who abuse alcohol (emphasizing that self-referrals will be treated confidentially and not punished)
- Caution in imposing suspension or expulsion for violators, because students who are away from school and unsupervised may spend the time drinking alcohol

### Community Strategies

Communities, as well as state and national governments, have a responsibility to protect families and children by promoting laws and attitudes that control alcohol consumption. Communities that minimize the visibility and availability of alcohol also help minimize the underage drinking problem. Teen alcohol consumption is less likely when advertisements and promotion of alcohol is curtailed or eliminated from public view. Surveys indicate that 96 percent of adults polled in America are concerned about underage drinking and would support efforts to reduce the risks. What can we do as parents?

- Support and promote legal and judicial policies and programs.
- Promote and support nonalcoholic leisure and recreational activities.

- Support recreational and educational programs that provide healthy alternatives to teenage drinking.
- Support peer programs that emphasize social, communication, and life skills in teens.
- Work to eliminate alcohol-sponsored community activities.
- Work to curb community tolerance for alcohol abuse at any age.
- Promote open communication and discussion in the community regarding issues and concerns of teenage drinking.

## Diversion

As we learned earlier, alcohol is a significant attraction for teens. We also learned that alcoholism is a progressive disease, beginning with experimentation and progressing through phases of abuse, dependence, and addiction. When prevention has not fully worked and a teen begins to experiment with alcohol and perhaps to have early problems because of use, diversion can assist in helping to correct the problems. Diversion simply means to divert attention away from something undesirable that has become intriguing or a potential problem.

A diversion program is *not* an alcohol treatment program. It normally does not involve a residential or even a partial residential stay. It can be done in the home, in a school setting, or in any other setting. It is designed as an "early warning" system for teens who are headed for problems with alcohol and alcohol-related behavior, but who aren't there yet. Diversion programs help adolescents understand the dangers associated with alcohol use, and they discourage alcohol-related behavior by encouraging youth toward healthy growth and development and by helping them discover personal resources and a positive direction in life.

Through the use of workbooks, workshops, and group and family activities, these programs help families mobilize around at-risk teens to find alternatives to or diversions from alcohol abuse. Such programs involve the teen, parents, other family members, other people, and facilitators. Remember that diversion programs seek to do more than help teens recover from alcohol abuse. They also help them develop life interests, skills, relationships, behaviors, and attitudes that "divert" the focus from alcohol abuse to more productive endeavors.

### How Can I Tell if a Diversion Program Is for My Teen?

Diversion programs are not used for addiction or dependence. That requires treatment intervention. However, if a teen has shown an infatuation with alcohol and has begun to experiment, even to misuse alcohol, a diversion program may be a good choice. Think of it this way: our teen is traveling on a road toward a destination. The train he is on is coming to a junction in the road. One track leads toward the town of Happiness; the other to the twin cities of Abuse and Addiction. Our teen is showing excitement and interest in taking the train to the twin cities. In fact, he has made friends with others who are headed there, and he is already drinking. You desire to divert him from his destination and get him on the train to Happiness. Diversion programs are designed to do just that.

### What Will a Diversion Program Require of My Family and Me?

Regardless of what program we are talking about, prevention, diversion, or recovery treatment, our child needs her parents and family. Diversion programs show a high rate of success when families are involved. As parents, we are an important part of the success of this program. Even if we feel that our teen is distant and resistive, we still remain an important role model and facilitator for her growth. Parents and families are typically asked to participate actively in family groups, family homework assignments, and family exercises and activities with a facilitator.

### What Does a Diversion Program Look Like?

By way of example, let's consider a program that was developed by Laura Burney Nissen, Ph.D., M.S.W., and that was published by Hazelden Foundation. *Alternate Routes* is a strength-based approach to helping teens who have begun to have problems with alcohol. Instead of focusing on the negatives and failures of teens, the program emphasizes the good and the positive aspects of teens. It "identif[ies] and celebrat[es] strengths, building on them, and then creat[es] new expectations to reshape their lives. The genius of a strength-based approach is that youth—many for the first time—begin to believe in themselves. They are empowered by being praised and encouraged and rewarded."[3]

The program contains a family guide, a teen guide, and a facilitator's guide. The guides help the teen and family members focus on twelve specific aspects of a diversion program:

1. Changes: Recognizes change as natural and positive, and empowers them to make planned changes that are positive.
2. Identity: Helps teens explore themselves and form an image of how they would like to be.
3. Responsibility: Helps youth identify their rightful responsibilities in life and form strategies on how to successfully meet them without the use of alcohol.
4. The Role of Alcohol: Helps youth identify warning signs of problems with alcohol, examine their attitudes and behaviors, and access help.
5. Relationships: Helps youth explore relationships and cultivate healthy relationships without alcohol.
6. Vision: Safely explores goals and ways to achieve these goals without alcohol.
7. Reaching: Helps teens learn to make positive decisions in

their lives to reach the goals that they feel are worthwhile.

8. Spirituality: Helps youth consider the spiritual dimension of their lives and accept concepts such as gratitude, morality, and spirituality in their lives.

9. Justice: Helps youth consider concepts of justice and fairness in their lives, and how their choices contribute to problems and solutions.

10. Gifts: Helps youth explore their strengths and weaknesses, strengthening self-esteem and hope.

11. Fun: Explores fun from both a positive and negative, low- and high-risk point of view. Helps teens establish balance in work and play.

12. Focus: Helps teens stay on track to their goals and get back on track when they get off.

Diversion plans help identify, explore, and develop from a strength-based point of view, rather than from a negative or needs point of view. Diversion asks, "What are your strengths and what can you bring to the table that will help?" instead of "What are your weaknesses and needs?" It helps teens empower themselves and make and follow a plan. Parents and other family members become involved in a way that helps everyone.

Diversion programs are relatively new but are achieving increasing popularity and use throughout the United States. You can check with your school counselor or professional services in your community or state for such programs.

# Chapter 8

# Intervention:
# How Parents Can Help Teens

$T$his chapter will address intervention—how and what parents can do to approach their children regarding alcoholism and to get appropriate help. Intervention is the step that precedes treatment. Convincing our child that she needs treatment may be as easy as sitting down and having a heart-to-heart conversation. More likely, our child will deny our accusations. However difficult it may be to talk to our child about what we believe is happening to her, we need to keep in mind that we are still the parents and that our child's welfare is our responsibility. An intervention may be hard, but the road ahead will be even rougher if we pretend everything will just get better if we leave it alone.

Teens are not adults. That is, they are not fully mature mentally or emotionally, and they are still dependent upon parents and society, although they like to think they aren't. They need parents' help. Treatment for alcoholic teens has been proven time and again to be far more effective when teens have the positive and loving support of parents and other family members. Unfortunately, by the time a teen comes into treatment, the pain and resentment and rift between parents and teen is often so large that they don't want anything to do with each other. Lack of support is one of the great inhibitors in successful teen treatment and recovery. Support is needed before treatment even begins, during the crucial period when parents need to have the courage to intervene or to let their child know they believe he has a serious problem with alcohol and why. A successful intervention requires some preparation and the proper mind-set.

## Breaking Our Own Denial

We may be in denial about our teen's drinking problem and not be able to see clearly our role in the problem or solution. In other words, we may be in denial as much as our teen. We may not have honestly faced the fact that our teen is an alcoholic or headed in that direction. We may still think that it's going to pass soon and everything will return to its proper state. We may be unwilling to face the heavy price we and our family, as well as our teen, have paid for problems with alcohol. We may blame the problem on others or on circumstances beyond our control. We may blame it all on our teen, feeling that it is his fault and that he has to fix the problems himself. We may not see the role that we and our family have played in helping to cause or continue the drinking problem. We or another member of our family may use or abuse alcohol and be unwilling to admit the problems it causes for us, our family, and particularly our teen's view of his use.

Denial can be extremely difficult to see, face, and break. It takes honesty and humility in us and our teen. It is so easy—so tempting—to blame our child and exonerate ourselves, and to see the changes so desperately needed in her life and ignore those in our own. The Bible's gospel of Saint Luke calls this the mote and the beam principle. The truth is, when our teen is suffering from alcoholism, everyone in the family needs to recover in some way. My experience tells me that the sooner we break our own denial, the better chance our teen has to break his denial and get into treatment and recovery. We may need to find someone we can trust who has the skills to help us honestly and objectively look at our role in both the cause and the solution to the addiction problems we face with our teen. We need to ask some diffi-cult questions of ourselves: How do we contribute to the problem? How can we contribute to the solution? What do we need to change in ourselves and our family to promote true recovery? What are we willing to do? Whom do we love most, our child or ourselves? These questions must be answered, not for the purpose of blaming or filling ourselves with guilt but to make us more aware, more humble, and stronger. Until we do, we may not be able to help our child.

## Feeding the Bear

When I was a boy living in Yellowstone, the park· had big problems with bears because people fed them. The bears got in the habit of beg-ging for food on the roadsides and coming into campgrounds at night looking for easy food. As long as people continued to feed the bears, the bears hung around and were a nuisance and a threat. The same is true with alcohol. As long as the teen continues to drink, he will never recover. There are at least three actions parents need to take to stop feeding the teen's addiction:

### Stop the Drinking

The need to feel intoxicated is one of the driving forces of alcoholism. It does not work to try to cut down or slow down when addiction is the problem. Our teen has already tried and failed at "controlled" drinking. A continuation of drinking reinforces the strong cravings and physical dependence. The only way to interrupt the addiction is to stop drinking alcohol and to allow the brain chemistry in the cen-tral nervous system to regain some sense of normalcy without the presence of alcohol.

Willpower isn't strong enough to deny physical cravings and the pain of withdrawal. Promises, commitments, and good intentions get broken again and again. If we want the bear to go away, we must help our teen to stop feeding it *completely*. I am not suggesting that we, as parents, should quit our jobs and monitor our child 24/7. I am suggesting that our addicted teen is likely not going to quit on her own, and she is likely going to resist our initial attempts at regaining control. Our teen may require detoxification to rid her system of the influence of alcohol, followed by some type of treatment to help her change pro-alcohol beliefs, attitudes, thoughts, feelings, and relationships that put her at high risk for relapse. We have to decide where and how we can best help our teen stop feeding the addiction, and it is crucially important to realize that abstinence must be a number one priority.

## Change Relationships

As long as our teen can access the people, places, and things that provide alcohol and sustain his drinking habits, he will continue to drink. Drinking friends will actively promote drinking by encouraging, pleading, and even threatening him. Places where our teen drank or that remind him of alcohol will prompt cravings. Objects, including posters, pictures, music, beer mugs, and certain clothing, can also serve as reminders that resurrect the desire to drink alcohol. An abusing teen may be able to make changes within his environment. An addicted teen will likely not be able to make needed changes on his own and may need a change of residence long enough to reduce the craving and regain some control. Simply trying to force our teen to change friends and activities can be arduous and exhausting, and often not very productive. Some parents resort to moving to another place or sending their child off to live with a relative. Changing environments is helpful to some, but it's not usually enough because the teen takes the addictive thinking and feeling with him wherever he goes, and he will find what he is looking for in almost any place on earth. Our teen needs to change the inner and outer relationships he has with alcohol, with people, and with family members. I will say more about this later in discussing treatment, but let me emphasize here that the relationship our teen maintains with alcohol and the factors that enable continued drinking are the most critical things to change if we hope to have a successful outcome. The home environment is one of the most important factors.

### Stop Rationalizing

If we have allowed our teen to drink or have been tolerant of it, this must stop. Rationalizing and justifying alcohol use only promotes it. Even a passive, laissez-faire attitude on our part will enable our teen to drink. The first realization we need to come to is that our addicted teen cannot be around alcohol without eventually falling to the temptation to drink. This means that we, as parents, need to decide what role we will play. It seems self-evident that we must be absolutely loyal to our teen's abstinence from alcohol, but there remains the question of our own use of alcohol and having alcohol in the home. At the outset of this book, I said that I would never tell an adult not to drink alcohol. I am now simply asking parents to consider and constructively resolve the problem that arises in a home where parents drink—even moderately—and an alcoholic teen is trying to recover.

## Confronting the Problem

The ostrich approach to solving teenage alcoholism doesn't work. We can't bury our heads in the sand and hope it will go away. We will need to confront our teen about the drinking problem and the need for professional help. Timing and method are important with teens.

### Timing

Delaying the confrontation only worsens the problem and puts off the inevitable. We need to get appropriate support, choose a time and place, and act as soon as we suspect or have proof of a drinking problem. Suspicions should be discreetly investigated until there is ample proof. Falsely accusing our teen will only damage our relationship. But procrastination is also dangerous because it can give our teen a green light to continue abusing, and often time is of the essence.

It is easier and more effective when we have the support of fellow parents, teachers, administrators, and other professionals in confronting the problems. Parents can organize within a school or neighborhood, watching out for each other's children and reporting. Teachers, peers, friends, school officials, police officers, clergy, and other sources can help. The more eyes that see and report, the more timely and effective the response we can give. How often have we seen tragic incidents where lives were lost or ruined because several people—especially friends and peers—knew of problems but either weren't asked or didn't feel it necessary to say anything?

### Manner

We need to speak in a manner that promotes open, honest communication rather than denial and deceit. We want our child to talk with us, not lie to us. Waiting until we are under extreme pressure and approaching with anger, disgust, or great emotion serves only to charge the situation with negative feelings that will widen the gulf between us and our teen. We can choose words and a tone of voice that promote mutual respect, calmness, and caring, but absolute resolve. Avoid split feelings between parents. Both must send the same message. As in prevention, we can enlist other important people to send a similar message, or at least not undermine each other. The more our teen hears the same message, the more inclined she will be to accept it. We may need to talk it out first with a trusted confidant who can give us positive coaching. However we do it, we need to come to the table with a calm and firm resolve.

We are dealing with a teen who is addicted to alcohol. Addiction is a disease of denial and refusal. Our teen may try several techniques to throw us off or push us away. She may even try promises. We cannot rely upon any of these from our addicted teen. Our child may already feel guilty or ashamed of her drinking, and she may be reticent to talk, presenting an attitude that ranges from disinterest or boredom to defensiveness or anger. We must be persistent in moving her into a discussion, not being frightened or rebuffed by her defenses. We can use our leverage as a parent, and do it respectfully and firmly. Earlier in this book we discussed ways to intervene without interfering. Let's review this approach in terms of confronting the problem head-on:

- *I care:* Make it clear that you care about and love your child and, for that reason only, you are addressing the issue of alcohol abuse. Rise above the anger, resentment, fear, and pain perhaps caused by the teen's alcoholic behaviors, and recognize that you care enough to help your teen fight against the disease that grips her.

- *I see:* Present facts about his problems (signs, behavior, moods, relationships) in a clear, firm, and resolved manner. Be specific: you have seen him actually drink, someone else has seen him drink and reported it to you, or you have seen evidence of drinking, such as beer cans or bottles or the smell of alcohol. Present this as factually as possible. Example: "John, I was downtown last night and I saw you and three of your friends going into a bar." Or "John, I found two beer cans in the bushes outside of your room, and your room smells of alcohol," or "I found residue of vomit that smells like alcohol on your clothes." Or "John, the principal told me today that you were drinking alcohol during noon hour." Ask him if he thinks he has a problem. Expect denial and do not be dissuaded. Ask him to give details or explain. If he refuses, be clear about what you have seen and know.

- *I feel:* Ask your child how she feels about the problem as she sees it or as you have described it to her. Again, expect denial, but encourage your child's expressions. Tell her how you feel about it and why. Be honest with the feelings, but don't act them out in demeanor. Acting out your emotions is self-serving and only lessens the chance of communication. It may be necessary for you to express your feelings to a friend or professional counselor before confronting your teen. An example of positive expression is "Mary, I have very strong feelings about you drinking alcohol. I feel (hurt, unsafe, threatened, or fearful)." Draw out and listen to her feelings, allowing her the right to feel and trying to understand those feelings without negative reaction, but do not allow your feelings of resolution and help to be dissuaded.

- *I want:* Ask your child what he wants to have happen. State the need you have and the desired behavior you want in your child. Be clear and exact about what you want; don't equivocate or generalize. It is important that you also listen to your child. He sees and feels and wants, also. Effective communication is both listening and speaking openly and honestly. An alcoholic child will likely not be able to speak with complete honesty, but you *can,* and you can help him achieve greater honesty by being forthright and firm. If you fail to speak and listen effectively, you fail to communicate. Failed diplomacy always results in armed conflict. Be prepared for your child's negotiations, manipulations, promises, and threats. Don't allow your child's wants, which may be just to avoid the problems, to dissuade your commitment to resolve the problems.

- *I will:* Ask your child what she is willing to do about it. Then, tell her what you *are* going to do. No threats, just facts that you will back up with action. Actions you can take include invoking consequences that have already been laid down for such behavior, withdrawal of trust (not love) and privileges that come with trust for a reasonable period of time, talking with parents of other teens involved, requiring restitution or proper amends for behaviors, and seeking assistance from professionals and/or a treatment program. Your resolve to act may be met with great distress from your teen, accompanied by tears, pleadings, promises, and even threats of running away or hating you for the rest of her life, or getting back at you in some way. These are not easy to endure, and it is helpful to have other adults and professionals to support you during this time. The important thing is to hold firm and not be pushed into inaction or retreat. Following through will require courage and resolve. Depending on your child, you may find it necessary to avoid saying exactly what steps you are taking to resolve or help with the problem. It may be necessary just to act and explain later when the child is in recovery.

### Deciding When to Intervene

If our teen is addicted to alcohol, we will need to directly intervene and take control because, typically, alcoholic teens have lost balance and control in their lives. Taking control is especially necessary when the health and safety of our child, our family, and other people are at stake. The sooner our teen gets into treatment, the better his chance is for recovery. Our child's health, happiness, and even his life will depend upon our intervention if he is addicted or abusing alcohol seriously. Other people may want to simply label our teen as a bad apple, a social reject. Others may want to blame and punish. Still others may simply deny the problem and deny that they have any responsibility to help. Nothing is gained by that behavior. Our child needs us as an advocate and a helper, not a blame-layer.

### Taking Control

If we must take control of our teen's life, we can do so with sensitivity and kindness, but with absolute firmness and resolve. We cannot equivocate or try to rationalize our behaviors with an addicted teen. Addiction is not a rational disease. We cannot be a "bleeding heart" when it comes to addiction, or the disease will walk right over us. Taking control takes courage and fortitude and support. We sometimes must take control and then attempt to explain our actions when our teen is sober and rational enough to understand.

By taking control, I mean getting our teen into meaningful treatment or care that will begin the process of recovery by accessing and activating resources—professional and otherwise—to structure our teen's life to achieve recovery. I mean temporarily taking the power to make decisions about using alcohol out of our teen's hands and into our own and those of the professionals we have enlisted to help. I also mean that we, as parents, regain absolute control of our home and what happens there. We have neither the time nor the resources at home that it takes to gain control of an out-of-control teen, but professionals do. We must decide just how much control is needed.

Our goal must be to help our child regain control, never to maintain control forever. It is helpful to tell our teen that we have no intention of wanting to control her life but are taking control for a short time to help her regain control of her life without alcohol. Expressing confidence in her, always leaving the responsibility on her shoulders, we let her know that we are there, willing and ready to help her. We must always speak with her and treat her in ways that reflect our respect, confidence, and sense of her personal worth.

Our first task will probably be *to control ourselves* so that we don't speak and behave in harmful and irrational ways. If we have been dealing with an abusing or addicted teen for any length of time, we are probably at our wits' end. We will need to gather our faculties and emotions, make a plan, and then proceed with courage. If we feel that our own life is out of control, we can benefit from involving other adults we trust to help while we are getting our life under control. If we haven't been involved in our teen's life much up to this point, we are going to somehow have to explain why we weren't involved and why we now want to be involved. That may even be one of the reasons our teen is abusing alcohol. If so, we have some fence mending to do.

Another task of control is, of course, *to find the right professional and support resources*. There are many with varying levels of competency and philosophy. We'll talk more about that in the treatment section.

A third task is *to support our teen* and to do what we can to promote a successful outcome. Part of this includes making needed changes in ourselves and preparing our home environment to be supportive to sustained recovery.

Most addicted teens do not come to the table of abstinence willingly, especially when there has been significant family turmoil and trouble. If our teen was well adjusted up to the time that he became addicted to alcohol, recovery might come easier than if our teen has long-standing emotional, psychological, and behavioral problems in addition to the addiction. Long-term behavioral and psychological problems may have prevented bonding or the development of close relationships. Our teen may lack the skills necessary to recover. The challenge of recovery can be more difficult because more dynamics are at play. If this is the case, we will most likely need the help of trained professionals.

## Calling 911

In deciding when to call for emergency help, the overriding consideration is whether our child's life is in imminent danger from an overdose of drugs. Remember that drugs, including alcohol, can kill. Hundreds of college-age students die each year from alcohol poisoning or toxicity caused by binge drinking. If our child is unconscious due to the use of alcohol (this does not mean sleeping off a hangover but actually unconscious), we need to call 911 immediately and seek emergency medical treatment. It is also useful to search the area for clues or, if the person is conscious, to ask him what he took and how much and to get useful detailed information.

## Involving Police

It is illegal for an adult to sell alcohol to or to buy alcohol for a minor. It is illegal for a minor to buy alcohol from anyone and to use false identification to do so. Police should become involved in any case where we suspect or have proof that serious misdemeanors or felonies have occurred, especially when safety and life have been jeopardized. To wink at or close our eyes to this type of behavior only serves to perpetuate the social problems in our community.

# Chapter 9

# Treatment: The Next Step

---

**S**uccessful intervention must result in effective treatment. It is the parents' job to help get their addicted teen into the meaningful care of professionals who can help begin the treatment process and move the teen toward recovery. Treatment for alcoholism or other drug dependencies requires skills achieved through education and training. Professionals who understand teens, drugs, alcoholism, and effective tools to combat the disease are ready to help. Some parents are reluctant to get treatment for their teen. Somehow, they believe that treatment implies weakness, that they couldn't solve or manage their own problems or those of their family members. I believe that reluctance to get help is usually self-serving, stemming from personal embarrassment, fear of being exposed, not taking the problem seriously enough, a lack of knowledge, or hopelessness.

### Can Alcoholism Be Cured?

There is currently no known cure for alcoholism. Once the disease of addiction is activated by the abuse of alcohol, a person remains susceptible to alcoholism for the rest of his or her life. However, alcoholism does not need to destroy a person or prevent him or her from living a healthy life. It just means that a person cannot safely use alcohol or other mood-altering drugs.

Scientists are seeking cures through genetic research, but even if a medication or operation is discovered to deactivate genes that cause addiction, it stands to reason that alcohol will always have potentially dangerous effects upon people, especially teens.

Alcoholism is not the only disease without a known cure. There are others: forms of cancer, heart disease, diabetes, and so on. Although we can't outright cure these diseases, we are learning ways to prevent some of them by the avoidance of high-risk behavior.

For example, we know that nicotine in tobacco is an actual cancer-causing substance (carcinogen) and that by avoiding its use we can significantly reduce our chances of contracting certain types of cancers that are connected to smoking. We believe, also, that alcohol is a cancer-enhancing substance when combined with other known carcinogens, such as nicotine. That is, it increases the likelihood of getting cancer and speeds the growth of cancer cells in a victim. We can greatly decrease our chances of certain types of cancer by avoiding both tobacco and alcohol.

## Can Alcoholism Be Successfully Treated?

Happily, alcoholism is treatable. No teen or family member suffering from alcoholism or alcohol abuse need remain forever miserable or doomed to an early grave. There are proven ways to successfully help children recover from alcoholism, but it takes effort and some changes in the way we think and act.

There are reasons why some teens do not recover from alcoholism, and they have nothing to do with the severity of the disease or the myth that it is untreatable. Continued alcoholism and relapse—the recurrence of active drinking—occur because the teen and the family don't do what it takes to recover. There are proven, effective methods of treatment, and a teen can recover from alcoholism and live a healthy, happy life, provided she does what is necessary.

A comparison of alcoholism to diabetes will illustrate my point.

Most cases of diabetes can be successfully controlled through appropriate diet and medication. Most diabetics live healthy, productive lives. This does not mean that diabetes has gone away. On the contrary, diabetes will become active again if the diabetic stops taking medication or ignores diet restrictions. Most diabetics need not suffer life-threatening symptoms if they follow proper treatment protocol. Similarly, the alcoholic will never be rid of the addiction to alcohol, but it can be successfully controlled with appropriate lifestyle and behavioral changes.

### What Resources Can Help?

Help is available right in our community from professional, religious, and community services. There are also state, regional, and national organizations that will help. Most, if not all of these, can be found in the telephone directory. Here are some sources of information:

National organizations dedicated to helping with alcoholism and recovery include the following:

*Al-Anon Family Group Headquarters, Inc.*
1600 Corporate Landing Parkway
Virginia Beach, VA 23454-5617
Phone: 1-757-563-1600 (1-800-4AL-ANON for meeting information); e-mail: WSO@al-anon.org
Web site: www.al-anon.org

*Alcoholics Anonymous (AA) World Services, Inc.*
475 Riverside Drive, 11th Floor, New York, NY 10115
Mailing address: Grand Central Station, P.O. Box 459
New York, NY 10163
Phone: 1-212-870-3400
Web site: www.aa.org

Local chapters of these organizations are found in your telephone directory.

Organizations that provide information about alcoholism and other addictions include the following:

*National Council on Alcoholism and Drug Dependence, Inc. (NCADD)*
20 Exchange Place, Suite 2902, New York, NY 10005
Phone: 1-212-269-7797, e-mail: national@ncadd.org
Web site: www.ncadd.org

*National Institute on Alcohol Abuse and Alcoholism (NIAAA)*
6000 Executive Boulevard, Willco Building, Suite 409
Bethesda, MD 20892-7003
Phone: 301-443-3860, e-mail: niaaaweb-r@exchange.nih.gov
Web site: www.niaaa.nih.gov

*Hazelden*
P.O. Box 11, Center City, MN 55012-0011
Phone: 1-800-257-7800; e-mail: info@hazelden.org
Web site: www.hazelden.org
Hazelden provides residential and outpatient service and has a network system to help alcoholics. Of course, there are many other quality programs that also treat alcoholism; some of these partner with Hazelden and some do not, but a representative there can help you.

Local community resources can be found right in the telephone directory:

- Family doctors
- Community public health resources

- Professional counselors for addictions
- Local chapters of AA and sponsors
- Church clergy
- Local police agencies

### What Should I Consider When Seeking Help?

We deserve competent and appropriate assistance. We need to understand the types of care available and some key considerations before making a choice. Too many children and parents bounce from one care program to another until financial assistance has completely dried up, and they are no better off than when they started, sometimes worse. The following are helpful considerations in seeking help:

1. What are the presenting symptoms of our teen? Abuse? Dependence?
2. What level of crisis is our child currently experiencing?
3. What psychological and emotional problems exist besides addiction?
4. What is our teen's level of cooperation or resistance to recovery?
5. What is our home environment and family dynamics like?
6. What are the conditions of our neighborhood, community, and school?
7. What access does our teen have to positive, sober friends?
8. What level of spiritual support is available from church or other groups?
9. What was our relationship like with our teen before and during abuse?
10. Is there use or abuse of alcohol by other family members in our home?

11. How willing are family members to be involved in the treatment process?
12. Does our teen possess adequate social and life skills?
13. What is the age and maturity level of our teen?
14. What amount of structure will be required to recover?
15. What can we afford in terms of treatment?
16. What resources are available to us?
17. Will my teen benefit by living at home while undergoing treatment?

## What Level of Care Is Needed?

The level of care depends upon the level of need. It's that simple. The best way to know the level of need is to get a thorough, broad-based assessment from a trained professional. It saves time, resources, and personal pain. Almost every community has professionals trained in assessments, and some treatment facilities offer assessment services as well. A meaningful assessment must be more than just about alcohol abuse. A close look at many aspects of a teen's life can show problem areas that may have led to and will sustain high risk for abuse.

A good assessment should include the following:

- *Alcohol and other drug use patterns:* Drug use patterns are revealed in when drug use began, when it worsened, unsuccessful attempts to cut back or quit, increased use over time, switching from one drug to another, multiple use of drugs, physical and mental consequences or symptoms of use, when drinking occurs, whom with, how much, and its impact on life.
- *Behavior patterns:* Behavior patterns help professionals see the relationship of behavior to alcohol. They will need to understand behavior prior to drinking and since beginning drinking. They will want to know displayed patterns of aggression, anger,

threats, and physical altercations; irritation, annoyance; stealing, dishonesty, and lying; changes in eating and sleeping habits.

- *Social patterns:* Our teen's activities, interests, peer groups, close friends, and other associations, as well as ability to find and sustain social relationships and friendships, are important indicators to profe... nals about the role alcohol plays in our child's life and sub...quent recovery. This information will help professionals work more effectively with our child in treatment, but also help us make plans for continued sobriety and personal growth after active treatment has ended.

- *Academic patterns:* The school environment is an important truth teller in a child's life, and professionals need to understand what role alcohol and other psychological, social, and behavioral problems have played. They will want to know whether our child has experienced increased difficulty in school: truancy, difficulty in getting up and going to school, poor grades, not doing assignments, tardiness, apathy toward schoolwork, conflict with peers at school, conflict with teachers and school administrators, and suspensions and/or expulsions from school.

- *Psychological and emotional patterns:* As we have seen earlier, psychological and emotional problems often play a large role in our teen's alcohol problems. Professionals look for problems with mood stability; learning disabilities; adjustment problems; maladaptive ways of coping with life and emotions; suicidal thoughts or attempts; developmental milestone abnormalities, including emotional, mental, and physical; trauma that may not be resolved; and other mental problems, such as retardation (mild or otherwise).

- *Value orientation:* A teen's value structure tells a lot about his inner character and how successful treatment will be in helping him achieve and maintain a clean and sober lifestyle. Teens possessing relatively few or no moral values or sense of right and wrong will need to acquire them if they are to sustain recovery. Professionals will assess the values of our teen prior to the onset of drinking and afterward, family values and standards, religious or spiritual value structure, and sense of right and wrong, good and bad.

- *Family patterns:* Family patterns in a child's life tell a lot about the role and persistence alcohol may play in a child's life and possibly why alcohol became a problem in the first place. Professionals will consider our child's position in the family; whether our child is biological or adopted; early childhood experiences; relationships with parents and siblings prior to the onset of drinking and subsequently; boundaries, limits, and disciplinary techniques; communications; and parental roles and bonding.

We may feel that this assessment is getting too personal and that no one has the right to know some of this information. We may also fear that it might result in our family being blamed for problems and having to make some changes. The parent side of me empathizes. The therapist-counselor side of me says: Why waste our money and time and the life of our child by playing a guessing game? Let's get the facts and work together to solve the problems. When our family has bottomed out because of the hellish experiences of addiction, we will have no pride left; all we will seek is relief any way it can come. That is when we will not care about protecting our privacy as much as we will care about resolving the problem and returning to some normalcy. The earlier we come to this realization, the less we and our teen have to suffer.

After working for years with many addicted teens—and some who are seriously abusing drugs—I feel it safe to say that a majority of them feel relieved when the decision is finally made and they are to go to

treatment. That doesn't necessarily mean that they weep with gratitude and become model clients. They are still very much under the
influence of alcoholic thinking and behaviors, and these subside only
with abstinence and counseling. Many also suffer from anger and attitudes of belligerence and behavioral and psychological problems that
further diminish their cooperation. Teens who are reinforced by an
antisocial peer group—such as a gang—can be even more resistant.
Nevertheless, a huge weight of fear and uncertainty is lifted from their
young shoulders, and for the first time—whether they let us know or
not—many of them begin to face reality and feel hope.

Getting a teen into treatment is a chore and is typically filled with
emotional and behavioral turmoil and desperate attempts at avoidance. Most teens aren't particularly good at taking responsibility for
their problems and tend to blame parents and others. Many struggle
mightily; others come with a calculating determination to ride it out so
they can go back to drinking later; still others come peaceably and with
good intentions. Measures for getting kids into needed treatment
depend upon the urgency of their circumstances and their level of
cooperation. We can receive assistance from professional counselors,
doctors, school administrators, and other public officials not only to
strengthen teens in their resolve but also to apply appropriate pressure
on our teens to do the right thing. Of course, when our teen's drinking
has become problematic enough, treatment may be mandated by a
judge. As parents, we can often feel alone with our problems, caught
between the defiant child and a society that seems all too ready to condemn us. We are not alone, and there are many support groups, parents'
coalitions, and professional people who will give good advice and help.

### How Do I Decide on an Appropriate Treatment Program?

Once we have determined the extent of the problem through a good
assessment, our next task is to find the tools and people who can really

help. Studies have shown that several different treatment approaches can be effective in promoting recovery, such as Twelve Step programs, cognitive- and behavior-focused programs, and motivational programs. Parents need to consider some important factors in choosing a program.

- *It is the least invasive and intrusive.* We need to select a program that is as unintrusive and unrestrictive as possible, that minimizes unnecessary trauma and feelings of abnormality. If increased support or structure is needed, we should not be afraid to make a change in program. For example, if an outpatient program just isn't working, we may decide upon a residential program or wilderness program. With the extreme costs of treatment, it is in our best interest to find what works earlier rather than later. Teens who get bounced from one program to another tend to get discouraged and hopeless.

  Some people feel that the less disruptive and traumatic a program is, the more easily a teen will adjust and the better she will do. I think that it is important to provide treatment that is sensitive, supportive, and respectful. However, some kids benefit significantly from rude awakenings and programs that are challenging—not brutal or inhumane. Sometimes a child needs to know that her behavior isn't normal, isn't appreciated, and won't be tolerated. Sometimes losing freedom and privileges—not human dignity—opens her eyes to a sense of reality and change that wouldn't come by protecting her so she doesn't feel "different" or "traumatized."

- *It meets the needs of our child.* The guiding principle is to treat, not punish; to motivate and cause positive insight and change, not incarcerate. A treatment program or regime must meet the specific needs of our child. Not every treatment program is right for every child. If our child needs to be out of the home, away from his environment, we need to find a program that provides proper structure and treatment. If our child is belligerent, oppositional, or defiant, in addition to being alcoholic, he may need a residential program that provides strict, consequence-based structure. Our child might benefit from a nature or wilderness program or an equestrian program. If our child would benefit most by being at home and we can provide the support needed, a day-care or release-time program would make that possible. A program should treat the causes and problems, should have the trained staff needed for this care, and should treat clients and families with respect and care.

In selecting a program, the priority is our teen's recovery, not our convenience or comfort. I've seen parents place their teen where it wasn't in the child's best interest but was convenient or comfortable for them. Perhaps they knew that they wouldn't have to be involved or make any changes. Perhaps it was less noticeable or less restrictive so they didn't feel guilty for what they were doing. Treatment is not about us, as parents, but about what is good for our children in need.

- *It includes parent and family involvement.* I believe that when it is possible, treatment should take place when and where parents and family members can provide direct support and encouragement to the teen. This is not always possible, especially in the early stages of treatment, because of out-of-control behavior and attitudes. Once the effects of the alcohol or other drug are out of the system and some stability has been achieved, the family needs to be involved.

- *It has a compatible theoretical approach and belief system.* We need to select a program that has a belief system and theoretical approach consistent with our basic beliefs and values. A note of caution is appropriate. It is possible that our belief system might be one of the problems or may not be the most effective way of dealing with the problem. For instance, a parent might believe that the Twelve Step program is some kind of cult approach to healing that requires a person to join a religion or accept God, and might be very uncomfortable with that. We can keep an open mind to alternative approaches to treatment and not dismiss them categorically without learning clearly what they are about. Twelve Step programs are not religious fanaticism, but logical, sensitive steps to healing that allow a patient to embrace whatever he chooses as a power higher than himself. Just because a program's approach is not a parent's approach does not mean that it doesn't have solid values.

- *It takes a strength-based approach.* A program should value the worth of each child and work from a strength-based approach to overcome problems. We need to avoid programs that have a detention or purely disciplinary mentality. While it's true that for some youth, strict structure and discipline are the only way to control behavior and get them to a point where they will accept help, a program must be something more than a "warehouse" or a prison. It must be able to move children beyond control and structure and get to the heart of the precipitating problems.

- *It provides important teen support services.* A teen typically comes into treatment with psychological, educational, emotional, social, spiritual, and physical needs, depending upon the level of treatment and the acuity of her problems. She may need medical and health assistance related to alcohol abuse, counseling and psychological testing, psychiatric services for prescription medications, recreation and leisure training, educational or vocational support services, life skills training, structured living, alcohol and drug treatment counseling and groups, and other specialty groups that educate, train, support, or promote change.

## Important Components of Treatment

Listed below are some components that I believe are important to a teen's treatment. It's essential to consult with a professional we trust before deciding on an exact treatment protocol.

### Detoxification

As noted earlier, the presence of alcohol or other psychoactive drugs in a teen's system sustains dependence and addiction. It is essential to the recovery process for the child to rid his body and mind of the alcohol so that he can begin to regain some normalcy in thinking and feeling. Alcohol does not typically linger in the system of a teen or have the same permanent effects as some other drugs, but it does change beliefs, attitudes, and thinking processes, and it will take some time for our teen to recover. Detoxification is a medical process of safely getting alcohol out of our teen's body system so that he can begin the process of recovering his life. It requires trained personnel and medical procedures to do it safely. It is not comfortable and can be dangerous. Detoxification alone is not recovery, but it is the first step to recovery. It must be followed up with a specific recovery treatment to help our teen make important changes in beliefs, attitudes, thinking, feeling, behaviors, and relationships that have been self-defeating and have enabled alcoholism.

### Doctor-Prescribed Medication

Doctors sometimes prescribe medication to help prevent a return to drinking once a teen is sober. Medications are typically given for more serious cases, such as patients who are dually diagnosed with various behavioral or psychological disorders. Some scientists question the usefulness or appropriateness of these drugs. Such medications include disulfiram (Antabuse) or naltrexone (ReVia). These take monitoring and follow-up by parents or other responsible adults. We cannot rely upon our teen to follow the treatment protocol, especially in the early stages of recovery. *Medications, by themselves, are not sufficient for recovery.* A teen can usually find ways to overcome or circumvent the medication protocols and return to drinking. While medications help to enforce abstinence, recovery requires not just abstinence but changes in thoughts, feelings, actions, and lifestyle.

### Crisis Care

Facilities exist to admit and treat teens for short-term periods when they are in crisis. These include detoxification and crisis management care to help the teen overcome suicidal thoughts and regain stable emotions and thinking. These facilities are typically more expensive and focus purely on stabilizing a child prior to release. These facilities can be lifesavers when a child is in crisis, but they are not meant for long-term treatment.

### Outpatient Care

Outpatient care typically allows the teen to live at home and continue a normal daily routine while coming periodically (one to three times a week) to the clinician's office for counseling or therapy. Most communities have trained professionals who provide drug and alcohol counseling for individuals, groups, and families. Sometimes these are private for-profit offices and sometimes they are government-subsidized or nonprofit organizations. Outpatient care does not normally work very effectively in the early stages of addiction treatment because of the teen's (and perhaps the family's) instability and resistance to help. It does, however, work extremely well for care once primary treatment is completed and the teen returns to live at home.

Outpatient professionals provide continuing support, structure, follow-up, and counseling.

## Day-Care Treatment

Some clients require more structure in their daily routine but not full-time residential care. In day-care treatment, clients typically spend the day or part of a day in the treatment center receiving structured support, groups, counseling, and other services. At night they return to their homes. Sometimes a client attends a normal school for part of the day and spends a few hours of release time at the treatment center. This offers a balance of good structure during the day, while the parents may be working, and home living. Provided that a family is supportive and attentive to the treatment needs of the teen and can provide a positive, structured environment, day-care treatment can be helpful. When families cannot provide needed structure or support, or when conflicts at home create stress for the teen, gains made during the day are usually compromised at night. Full day-care programs typically offer educational services, or they may correlate a student's academic work with the patient's school.

## Psychiatric Care

Psychiatrists prescribe and monitor medications for children with psychiatric problems, such as major depression, bipolar disorder, attention deficit hyperactivity disorder, and borderline personality. If our child has co-occurring disorders—that is, one or more psychological disorders that require medication in addition to alcohol addiction—then treatment becomes increasingly challenging. The psychiatrist must find appropriate drugs (medications) that maximize the control of the disorder while minimizing the addiction problem. Sometime in the treatment, our teen may need to begin a medication protocol in spite of addiction to alcohol or another drug. It's important that parents and teens understand the difference between taking addictive, mood-altering drugs and medications prescribed to treat a psychiatric problem. Most psychiatric medications are not addictive and can be fundamental to a teen's solid recovery.

## Residential Treatment

Residential facilities provide twenty-four-hour-a-day care, normally with a broad range of treatment: counseling; structure; discipline; medical, psychiatric, and psychological services; academics and vocational support; development of social and living skills; recreation, and leisure. Teens eat, sleep, study, socialize, and live at the facility. There are many types of residential facilities, ranging from moderate-secure to nonsecure treatment. Residential treatment can be very useful to help a teen regain control and balance in her life and put a plan of recovery into action. Residential treatment can also be useful for an alcohol-dependent teen when the home and neighborhood environment is not healthy and cannot provide the necessary structure or when a teen has demonstrated an inability to control herself in less restrictive environments. Length of stay should be carefully monitored and terminated when appropriate goals related to the problems have been achieved.

If we are considering a residential setting, it is to our advantage to visit the facility, learn its program (not just read the brochure), feel its atmosphere, and get acquainted with its staff. We need to ensure that our teen will be treated with dignity and respect and that the program is firm enough to promote the changes needed for recovery. For teens with purely an alcohol addiction, a short-term residential experience is beneficial. Teens who are experiencing co-occurring disorders may require a longer stay. Whatever the case, active parent and family involvement is crucial.

### Individual Counseling

Relationships mean everything in recovery, and a teen will benefit significantly from a therapeutic relationship with a professional counselor who can help him identify and work through important issues. If a teen has psychological issues in addition to alcoholism, a trained therapist can help integrate emotions, cognition, and behavior with recovery from the effects of alcoholism. An increasing number of professionals are jointly credentialed in both psychological and behavioral issues as well as chemical addiction. This can be an advantage, because the teen then has fewer people with whom he is required to establish a therapeutic relationship. The dual issues are typically linked, and one professional tends to have a better capacity to integrate them into the treatment protocol than when two or more must coordinate. This is not always the case, however, and some teens benefit from multiple contacts. A case can be made that "two heads are better than one."

### Group Counseling

A teen can benefit from group counseling with other teens who are also trying to recover. Groups serve not only to promote honesty and break down initial defenses but also to teach our child important skills and knowledge and offer caring support and encouragement from other teens. However, group activities can be too challenging—even harmful—for teens who lack the maturity or social skills or psychological capacities to work within a group.

### Recreation and Leisure Groups

These groups teach teens how to have positive fun in recreation instead of "hanging out" and drinking with friends. They teach leisure skills, develop interests, and help a teen discover important truths about herself and the world around her through recreational activities.

## Meditation

Meditation is a means of helping our child focus internally upon important issues of recovery. Prayer is a form of meditation. Our teen's world is chaotic. The life of a teen, especially an addicted one, is impulsive, driven, and crazy. Meditation brings a calm focus into a teen's life. Through motivating thoughts and sayings and in programmed, structured time, our child is taught to think and to receive inspiration for recovery. It is a time to forgive herself and others, to make amends, to plan goals and make commitments. However, most meditation related to addiction is meant to clear the mind to "listen to a Higher Power."

## Family and Marriage Counseling

Family counseling can be productive if our family is willing to become invested in the recovery process. Addiction, treatment, and recovery are influenced by the relationships a teen has with his parents and family. This is not just our teen's problem, and recovery requires more than just his efforts. Parents and family members play a crucial role in recovery by supporting, encouraging, talking, resolving, planning, and changing. Through sensitive marriage and family counseling, parents and families can discover for themselves what changes they need to make to make life better for them and to help their child recover from addiction. The family must change along with the teen if recovery is to be sustained.

## Medical Care

Our teen may have physical health needs that are related to prolonged alcohol or other drug abuse. These needs may include sexually transmitted or communicable diseases, rashes, trouble with memory, and even impaired functioning of some body systems and organs. The teen may also be more susceptible to colds and viruses. These needs should be treated competently and sensitively by trained medical professionals to give the teen a sense of being cared for.

### Academic Support
Whether our teen is in a residential setting for an extended period of time or in less restrictive programs, it is important that she continue educational pursuits without long delays. Often, after our teen regains sobriety, she finds a renewed interest in learning, reading, and school. Success in learning is a great self-esteem booster. Filling time with learning and growing helps fill the void created by the absence of alcohol and an alcohol-related lifestyle.

### Continuing Care
Is there life after treatment? Yes! Once our teen has successfully completed a treatment program and is clean and sober, the program should move into the second phase, sometimes called "aftercare" or "continuing care." This simply means that care continues after treatment in the form of support and self-help groups such as Alcoholics Anonymous (AA), continued counseling or therapy, medication protocols, and other activities that support a clean and sober lifestyle.

### Relapse Prevention Counseling
Relapse means returning to drinking once a teen is sober. Relapses can simply be slips, when the addict has a drink, or they can be total plunges back into active addiction. Relapse is common, especially among teens. Some figures place relapse at as high as 80 percent in teens trying to recover. Some teens relapse multiple times before ever going straight and sober. Relapse does not mean that treatment was a failure or that all is lost. Teens can and most frequently do rebound from relapses. Relapse is a testament to how difficult recovery can be.

Having said that, I want to emphasize that relapse is predictable and preventable. Our teen should be helped during treatment to iden-tify key warning signs or triggers of relapse. He should develop a per-sonal emergency relapse prevention plan that he can implement in crisis. Our teen should receive relapse prevention training from a counselor. If our teen relapses during recovery, which might well hap-pen, we and our child should have a plan to regain sobriety.

Relapse usually occurs for the following reasons:

- Failure to internalize important growth principles during treat-ment
- Failure to develop a meaningful, realistic recovery plan prior to discharge
- Failure to benefit from a positive support group
- Failure to follow a structured recovery plan at home
- Failure to thrive in the home environment

## Support Systems

Our treatment professionals should help us and our teen develop a strong continuing care plan and support system. From my experience in working with teens, I believe that a support system is extremely important, and a teen needs more than just the family. Family mem-bers may not understand the teen's issues and concerns surrounding the use of alcohol because they haven't experienced it. This is not to say that the family does not provide necessary support and love, but that special problems need special support. The teen and other family members can become involved in support groups to help them face and resolve concerns and remain strongly committed to recovery. Alcoholics Anonymous, Narcotics Anonymous (NA), Al-Anon, and other support groups can provide valuable resources to a teen if care-fully selected and used properly.

Alcoholics Anonymous groups are attended by people who not

only need support but are willing to give it, especially to newcomers. They provide a forum where honesty about addiction is reinforced and unconditional acceptance and support is provided. Teens listen to others talk about their challenges and accomplishments, and it brings perspective and a realization that they are not alone and that they can live a life in recovery. This is important for teens because so often their mentality is that no one else in the world has experienced what they are experiencing. A support group teaches teens that they and their disease are not unique and that they can successfully recover. Our teen is always given opportunity to talk about her personal challenges and achievements and to receive support and encouragement and praise for what she has done. She is recognized with medallions for periods of sobriety (thirty, sixty, and ninety days, six months, nine months, and a year). Support groups provide honest confrontation of our teen's weaknesses by people who are fully aware of addictive thinking and behavior and are not fooled. The support groups for parents and family members of addicts are also meant to give support, encouragement, and advice to people who are trying to live with an addict.

Sponsors come from this support group. These are people who are themselves in recovery and give willingly of their time and abilities to coach others through the difficult days of early recovery. They know the pitfalls and are able to forewarn our child as he goes about his recovery. They can keep him focused on his relationship with recovery. They are a first line of defense that our teen can call when he feels tempted to slip or is showing signs of relapse. They are special friends and mentors to our teen in recovery. I encourage parents and family members not to be put off or jealous about this relationship with a sponsor. Parents and family members have an important role to play, also. We would not be offended if our child called a medical doctor for a health problem or allowed that doctor to prescribe and treat him for an illness. Likewise, our child has emotional needs in recovering from addiction. A strong support *team* that is committed to sobriety is important.

## What Role Should I Play in Treatment?

Our involvement in our children's recovery and treatment program can significantly influence the outcome. Having worked in a treatment facility with children, I would suggest we consider doing the following:

### Getting Involved

Teens with strong parental and family involvement do much better in recovery than those without and have stronger, longer-lasting results. We know our child better than anyone else. We may not have the expertise and training to know how to handle treatment, but we can be very helpful in providing staff key information for assessments, evaluations, and planning. We can be a positive influence to support and encourage our teen. As we demonstrate to our teen that we are willing to work just as hard as he does and that we are willing to make needed changes, we will send a strong signal to our teen of encouragement and hope.

### Refraining from Blaming or Finding Fault

We are wise to look for solutions and to expect our teen to take responsibility for recovery and to keep sending that message patiently and firmly, not with finger pointing but with constructive dialogues that solve problems. For example, instead of bringing up endless lists of how our teen has violated us and made life a living hell, we can focus on how it was for her and how she feels about it. We can avoid flaring into anger or self-pity fueled by her barbs. Instead of allowing our teen to hook us into an argument over something that was done or that happened, we can focus on lessons learned and how we can all do it better next time. We can leave the responsibility with her but express our interest and hopes. When I was working in a residential treatment center as a therapist, parents would often call to talk with their child in my presence and all they did was go through a laundry list of questions that were more interrogation than interest in the welfare of their child. They were still allowing themselves to be the enforcer, the checker, the sheriff. They were still trying to find reasons to find fault or criticize or say, "I thought so," or "I told you so." After some coaching, they were able to see this and let go of it and say things like, "Well, I have confidence that you can solve that problem," or "Gosh! I'm sorry to hear about that," or "That must have been disappointing to you, but I know that you can succeed." When they learned to leave the responsibility with their child and stop feeling obligated and guilty, a huge burden was lifted and their teen usually began to take responsibility.

### Promoting Positive Relationships

Figure 4 shows a model of relationships common in a treatment setting. Three primary relationships exist in treatment: (A) between our child and us, (B) between the treatment staff and us, and (C) between the treatment staff and our child. All three are critical to success. All three should coexist in a healthy way. Each key player can directly influence the relationships for good or ill, or indirectly (as indicated by the arrows showing indirect force). We need to act in such a way that we promote positive relationships.

Relationship A: If the relationship between us and our teen is rocky and difficult at first, we need to be patient and long-suffering, not trying to force it but just letting it evolve. It's the *Field of Dreams* principle: build it and they will come, go the distance, ease his pain. We provide support and encouragement but do not rescue. We may

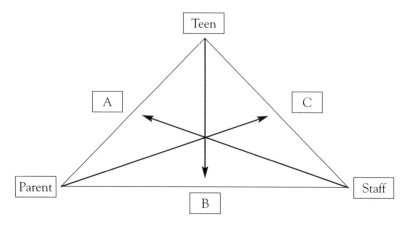

**Figure 4: Treatment Synergy**

first need to allow the relationship between staff and us and staff and our teen to grow before our relationship with our teen can become healthy. There is a good chance that the parent-child relationship will significantly improve over time.

Relationship B: The relationship between us and the treatment staff is important to the successful outcome of treatment. We need to give control over to the treatment staff and to assume a supportive role, not try to control the treatment program or the staff. That can be difficult if we are used to being in control. The trained staff need to be free to do their jobs. We should not allow our teen to split or sabotage our relationship with the staff by manipulation and should resist the temptation to become jealous and sabotage the relationship between our teen and the staff. If it's a positive relationship, we'll be grateful for it.

Relationship C: We need to encourage a healthy relationship between our teen and the staff, avoiding the temptation to become jealous or discouraged if our teen begins to respond in positive ways for the staff. A strong therapeutic relationship between our teen and a counselor can only help. As we remain supportive and active in the relationship, our influence will be felt and a healthy relationship between us and our teen can grow.

### Learning and Growing with Our Child

We cannot expect our teen to make all the changes while the rest of the family remains at status quo. In open discussion with the child's counselor or therapist, we learn what we can do to improve and to best help our child stay clean and sober. Proper counseling can help us to develop better parenting and communication skills, to understand our teen more, and to improve the family environment so that it is conducive to recovery. We need to be teachable. We need to be humble.

### Preparing a Healthy Home Environment

Our teen will either be living in our home during treatment or will probably return to live there when treatment is finished. The environment of our home, as well as the behavior of each member living there, will play a large role in supporting or harming the recovery process. Even if our child is in a good treatment program, coming back every night or after treatment is finished to a home that hasn't made any changes, that is filled with contention, discord, or parents and siblings who are using alcohol or other drugs, will guarantee a relapse. We have a responsibility to provide a healthy home environment.

### Making a Plan

While our teen is in treatment, we can work closely with her, the staff, and our family to develop a plan for sustaining sobriety and recovering a healthy lifestyle. A plan includes a mission statement; achievable, measurable, and meaningful goals; a healthy lifestyle plan; time management; stress management; and a personal emergency relapse prevention plan.

## Assembling a Support Team

We need to help our teen identify people who will provide a strong support team loyal to sobriety and recovery. This should include parents, siblings, extended family members, AA sponsor, counselor/therapist, doctors, teachers, other adults, and positive, sober peers.

## Empowering Recovery

Recovery from addiction won't just happen by itself and cannot be forced. We can lead our teen to water but we can't make him drink. However, we can help him discover and access powers that are necessary to recovery. Teens aren't friendly to the idea of powerlessness. It takes a teen a long time and considerable suffering to finally admit that he has lost control of his life and does not have the power alone to recover it.

By recovery, I don't mean just quit and relapse, quit and relapse, nor do I mean simply abstaining from drinking alcohol. More is required for our teen to recover a healthy life. Recovery begins with abstinence, true enough, but it must go beyond abstinence to filling in the holes with interests and pursuits that bring happiness, satisfaction, self-esteem, and success, something that alcohol had falsely filled before.

Let me reemphasize that abstinence alone does not mean happiness, but abstinence for an alcoholic is essential in order to find real happiness. Abstinence by itself usually leaves a teen feeling empty, sorrowful, lonely, ashamed, guilty, and fearful. That void must be filled with powers that bring true happiness. Recovery is more than just a goal or desired state, but a process of becoming. Our addicted teen will probably never return to the sweet preaddicted kid she was. She has grown and had experiences that have changed her. She will have new interests and discover new talents and abilities. She will have new ways of looking at things, new perceptions and insights. It is misleading for us to look for the emergence of the "old" kid from the fog of addiction. That kid is long gone. Look for a new and just as wonderful person to emerge.

# Chapter 10

# Recovery: Regaining a Healthy Lifestyle

Recovery does not mean cure; it means to "get back" or "regain a state of control, balance, good physical or mental health." Recovery does not mean that the teen or the family can continue with past behaviors and attitudes about alcohol that have enabled abuse in the past. It means consciously making needed changes and sustaining those changes.

Recovery *requires* that there be total abstinence from alcohol and other mood-altering drugs. An alcoholic teen cannot use socially or occasionally or under parental supervision. It is not a matter of careful judgment, timing, maturity, or determination. It is not a matter of a passing phase of life. It is a matter of physical dependence that never changes, even with age. Alcohol use will always reactivate a teen's craving for alcohol, often with even more power than before. If remission or recovery is not maintained, craving and active addiction will return.

Addiction causes a teen to lose control of his drinking and of his life. *Recovery* is the term used to indicate the state of control and equilibrium that is achieved when the influence of alcohol is taken away. This active influence of alcohol does not go easily. Its effects often linger in the form of obsessive thinking about, dreams about, and cravings for a drink, but these will diminish over time, and eventually, a teen can live without the persistent cravings that have made his life and ours a living hell.

The absence of alcohol leaves emotional and physical and social voids that must be filled with helpful replacements. These voids are not easy to fill because a recovering teen may have lost interest and a sense of pleasure in most positive endeavors. Depending upon how long alcoholism has been in the life of the teen, there may be lost time and skills to catch up on. With sustained effort, these voids can be filled and the teen can return to the normal, healthy lifestyle of a teen. Nevertheless, the disease remains forever buried in the brain's nervous system and cells of the body, and alcohol can make it come out of remission, even stronger than before.

### Recovering What Has Been Lost

It is worth repeating here that alcoholism robs a child of precious things, especially when its onset is early in adolescence. As we learned in a previous chapter, adolescence is a time of almost unparalleled growth, a time when significant achievements are programmed by nature's biological clock. Alcoholism disrupts this timetable, often creating voids and gaps that leave our child behind or disadvantaged.

Remember from our previous discussion that an adolescent makes significant growth and development in every part of her body. Allow me to summarize the losses that accompany alcoholism.

### Physical Losses

Teens are preoccupied with physical appearance. Body structure affects every aspect of a child: emotionally, in skills development, and in aptitudes. The body grows almost to its complete maturity during this period, gaining muscle and skeletal strength. The onset of puberty occurs in this period; reproductive systems develop. Alcohol is known to retard bone density and strength, muscle growth, and the development of reproductive organs and capacities in both sexes. It also negatively affects body organs and systems, causing various types of disease and enhancing viruses that can be dangerous.

### Cognitive Losses

Adolescence is a time for children to develop logical and complex thinking, allowing them to make rational decisions in a complex world. They begin to develop abstract thinking and are able to deal with hypothetical situations and draw inferences critical to adult performance. They become more philosophical, spiritual, and politically minded. Alcoholism stunts intellectual development and shrinks a teen's world into a narrow, shallow dimension of drinking and alcoholic relationships. An alcoholic often misses out on school, failing to develop important intellectual skills and to form fundamental knowledge basic to a productive life.

### Emotional Losses

Adolescence is a time of strong emotion and learning to control and resolve emotional issues. Alcoholism prevents that development by freezing everything under a drunk or a high. Alcoholic teens are frequently unable to deal with emotions or problems because they have hidden behind the influence of alcohol, leaving them unprepared for the demanding and complex relationships and challenges of the adult world.

### Social Losses

During adolescence teens learn to deal with sexual relationships, choose a career, and establish their own sense of identity. They do this primarily by relating with peers and others outside their family. They grow out of their egocentric self-absorption during this period and learn to be productive members of society. Often, alcoholic teens remain social children—preadolescent in their perceptions and outlooks. If they fail to find proper personal and social identity, they struggle to fit in, may become suicidal, or fall into negative patterns. Alcoholism stunts social development because it normally thrusts a child outside of healthy social patterns. They become outcasts or they spend their time romancing the bottle and drunks instead of developing social skills. They become known as "drunks" or "partiers" or "losers." Sexual and social relationships are stunted and contorted by alcoholism, leaving a teen undeveloped in sexual behavior, moral values, or ability to make and keep true friendships.

## Spiritual Losses

With abstract and complex thinking also comes the ability to decide and solidify what teens believe in spiritual terms, such as faith in God and trust and moral values. Most children begin with a simple and real faith in a Supreme Being. It is normal for a teen to begin to question what is real and imaginary in life and to make decisions about religion and God. Alcoholism allows only one god, itself, and squashes, for the most part, a trust or faith in anything other than the reality of drinking and the feeling of being drunk. Alcoholic teens almost always lose interest in God, in organized or personal religion, and usually feel so guilty and ashamed by what they do for the drug that they lose hope of ever being worthy—even if there is a God. Alcoholism causes spiritual bankruptcy. Spirituality and a belief in a Higher Power provide the most powerful lifelines for climbing up out of the pit of alcoholism and achieving recovery.

It is important for parents to recognize that alcoholism could come at no worse time in the life of a person than in adolescence. If a teen starts drinking at age thirteen or fourteen, quickly becomes an alcoholic, and drinks hard until sixteen or seventeen, he has literally lost three or four years of prime-time growth and maturation. Upon achieving sobriety, these skills don't just suddenly appear, as if they were somehow growing all the time under the deep freeze of alcohol.

Growth has been dormant during this period, and often an eighteen- or twenty-year-old finds that it is pretty tough to make it in the world when he's operating with the emotional, cognitive, and social skills of a fourteen-year-old.

Growth can and will come once sobriety is achieved, especially when the teen has recovered a healthy lifestyle. But often the lags in growth can be difficult to overcome and discouraging for teens who have missed out on many opportunities. Nevertheless, if they persevere, they can catch up, but it takes time and sustained effort.

### Lighting the Fire Within: Empowerment

It is a common saying within addiction circles, and a true one, that addiction is powerlessness over alcohol, or a loss of control. Indeed, recovery begins with an admission that we have lost control, that we are powerless over our addiction, and that life has become unmanageable. This realization leads us to an opening of ourselves to a Higher Power and to a humility that allows us eventually to recover. Powerlessness refers to being powerless over the disease, not over recovery. So when I speak of powers within a teen to recover, I mean that each human soul has the inherent potential to recover, to do something positive to achieve sobriety and happiness in life. If it were not so, our efforts would be meaningless. Temporary immobilization by addiction does not mean that our teen cannot discover and access the powers within her to recover. Powerlessness means that addiction has deprived our teen of the ability to recognize and use these powers, which now lie dormant, undeveloped, or covered up by alcoholism.

Powers that enable recovery come both from within and from without. Recovery must come in part from within a teen as he acts to gain sobriety and make positive changes in his life. Other powers for recovery come from outside: from other human beings and from an ultimately higher and more powerful source. Five essential powers are the power to see, the power to choose, the power to act, the power to heal, and the power to sustain recovery.

## The Power to See

Addiction is a disease of blindness and denial. The power to see helps remove the blindness and denial. It promotes honesty and acceptance of responsibility and help. A teen will not make the effort to recover if she does not honestly see and accept personal responsibility for her problem. She will never recover if she is not held accountable and responsible for that recovery. The power to see must come from within. We cannot force it or beat it into her. But we can influence it within her. We can recognize and accept personal responsibility for actions of our own that may relate to our teen's alcohol abuse. This modeling of behavior provides a good example for our teen to follow. We can make clear statements and draw clear lines of tolerance.

We need to be careful at this point that we don't hold our love or acceptance hostage by giving her a choice: alcohol or us. Alcohol will always win at this point because it has control. To access this power to see, we and our teen must achieve complete honesty. We must accept the reality of the problems, and we must gain knowledge about the problems we face. Honesty becomes the only policy.

### Honesty

Honesty implies humility. We need to face the truth instead of hiding behind lies, deception, and appearances. Fear, guilt, shame, distrust, discouragement, and habit inhibit honesty. We and our addicted teen must overcome these hurdles to honesty. Lying, deceiving, blaming, denying, and making excuses sustain the addiction. We can help our teen be honest with three simple techniques as we interact:

- Emphasize responsibility rather than blame or fault. Instead of saying to your child, "It is your fault that all of this happened," say, "It is your responsibility to do something positive to solve the problem."

- Focus on solutions, not causes. Dwelling on reasons why something happened is like "arranging chairs on the deck of the *Titanic*." True, we can learn from past mistakes, but more important is to find ways to prevent the ship from sinking or to save the lives of the people on the sinking ship.
- Be honest and demand honesty in return.

## Acceptance

Our teen needs to accept three important concepts in his life to begin recovery. These open the door to progress. As long as these doors remain shut, progress toward recovery cannot be realized. He accepts

- that he has a problem with alcohol and a responsibility to recover his life,
- that he is a person of worth despite the ugliness of addiction, and
- that he must accept help from others to recover.

Our teen may be good at demanding rights and privileges but slow to take the responsibility that comes with them. She still has a healthy amount of child in her, and not taking responsibility is typical of addictive thinking.

Recovery requires an acceptance of personal responsibility by our teen for his own behaviors, feelings, and thoughts and also for his recovery. It is harmful for us to try to force him to take responsibility for the disease or for actions of others over which he has no control or for which he is not responsible. For example, it is useless to blame our teen for an inherited weakness for addiction, just as it would be useless for us to blame ourselves for passing it on. It is profitable, however, for us and our teen to admit that we have the disease and to take personal responsibility for doing something about it: to take the steps to recover our lives. It is useless to blame the disease for the problems but profitable to hold ourselves and our teen responsible for attitudes, thoughts, and behaviors.

### Knowledge

Obtaining accurate information is important to seeing clearly and understanding this disease of addiction. Correct knowledge breaks down roadblocks to recovery, such as ignorance, hopelessness, helplessness, shame, grief, and guilt. Most addicted teens don't understand addiction or alcohol or why they have the problems they do. They often think they are a rotten black sheep of the family who can't do anything right. They don't understand addiction, how it works, where it comes from, and how they can recover. Learning about the dangers of alcohol, the disease of addiction, and themselves will help them understand and accept their situation and take responsibility for recovery.

### The Power to Choose

Our teen will begin to recover when she decides to recover. We cannot force or dictate our child's decision to recover with any lasting result. But we can help empower our teen to make a positive decision to recover.

I have known teens who knew they had a problem with alcohol or other drugs but weren't willing to do anything about it. They were willing to accept the belief that they would probably be dead by the age of twenty. There are reasons for such decisions. They have to do with a child's lack of hope, trust, self-esteem, and knowledge.

## *Hope (the Top-Down Principle)*

Discouraged kids are hopeless kids. Two things come to mind about hopelessness and addiction: First, recovery can appear awesome and overpowering. Giving up the habits and the cravings seem too difficult. Recovering what they have lost in the past and making amends for what they fear are unpardonable sins seems impossible. Second, the personal improvements they make seem meaningless if they see no change in anyone or anything else that has been part of the problem. I've had kids say to me, "Why should I try? My parents aren't making any changes. When I go home, it's going to be the same old problems. Nothing has changed in my neighborhood or school. . . . I'm still going to be seen as the same old troublemaker. Nobody's going to give me a chance." These thoughts squash hope. Parents can help elevate a teen's hope and vision for recovery. Let me illustrate with an example.

I remember climbing mountains with my father as a child. Standing at the bottom of an eleven-thousand-foot peak and looking up, I thought the possibility of getting to the top was hopeless. Nevertheless, I followed my dad through the forest. He taught me about the forest while we hiked. When I became discouraged, he coached me and helped me measure my progress upward. I followed my dad, pushing myself along, although at times I wanted dearly to turn around and go down. Eventually, we arrived at timberline, where we broke out of the trees high on the mountainside, and I could see the mountain summit above me and the world around me. Suddenly, I had my own vision and the momentum for climbing shifted from my father to me. Nothing could stop me from going upward. Then my father had to struggle to keep up with me. When we finally sat on the summit and looked at the path from the top down, it did not seem so daunting.

Our child may have to rely on us during the early phases of recovery, relying on our vision and our hope, until she gains her own vision. We can help our teen see the path and the steps that she must take to recover, and to see them from the top down, at least from our position higher on the path, by talking with her, sharing our point of view, and helping her see what we see. Lastly, we can help free her from the blinding discouragement of believing that nothing is changing around her, that the future is going to be a repeat of past problems and mistakes. It does not have to be so if parents and family will help pave the way.

## Circles of Trust

Alcoholism builds a love-trust relationship with the alcoholic that does not allow for other trust to exist. In some kids' minds, alcohol seems to be the only thing that hasn't let them down or hurt them. They can trust it to always do what it says it will do. Life and people in our child's life aren't always that trustworthy, and many kids struggle with that uncertainty. Recovery requires that our teen gain a good balance of trust in three areas that replace the trust he has had in alcohol: (1) himself, (2) other positive people, and (3) a Higher Power.

- *Trusting self:* Balancing trust is difficult for addicted teens. Addiction has often removed the opportunity for our teen to learn to trust herself. Her recent life (and perhaps more of her life) has been filled with a parade of mistakes, bad judgments, and "stupidity," and she bolsters herself by drinking and being with others who do the same. Sometimes the opposite is true, and a teen will develop a pseudoconfidence that is misguided and egotistical. They trust no one but themselves and exclude all other opinions. Alcohol often serves to maintain this rigid self-trust.
- *Trusting other people:* Trust of other people can also go to extremes. Sometimes, teens trust people too much or too little, and sometimes they simply trust the wrong people. Always, alcohol is a common denominator in our alcoholic teen's trust

equation. Our teen will need to learn to trust in self and other positive people without the use of alcohol. This will take time and practice, but we can help him to trust himself by coaching him to make positive choices. His first trust relationship needs to be with himself and his sobriety. All other relationships and decisions must support that.

- *Trusting a Higher Power:* The concept of a Higher Power frightens or turns off many recovering teens because they think that they are required to accept some religious belief or "bow down" to some god. Actually, the Higher Power concept as taught in the Twelve Step program of recovery has little to do with religion and everything to do with believing that there is a Higher Power than our own that cares about us and that can help us remove defects of character and recover from a life of addiction. Addiction to alcohol naturally destroys faith and interest in a Higher Power, especially something unseen or incomprehensible. So it is useful for our teen to understand that she is free to identify and choose her own Higher Power. There is an operative principle here that we must understand: A Higher Power must be higher and more powerful than our teen if it is to help lift her to recovery. It should not be herself, her parents, or her friends. This principle encourages a teen to develop a spiritual component to her life that is actually very powerful and important in true recovery.

I will finish this book with a more in-depth discussion of the healing power of spirituality. Suffice it to say that the Higher Power concept is an important exercise in spirituality, something from which our recovering teen will greatly benefit. Our teen may have difficulty picking something that requires faith, so he may begin with something tangible. We start where we are and hope it will grow into something more. If our teen has lost his trust or belief in a Higher Power, or if he never had one, we can help him cultivate this relationship. If we feel inadequate or unprepared to help our child learn that trust, we can promote it through other people. Whatever we do, we cannot discourage or sabotage our child's efforts in seeking spirituality and trust in a Higher Power. It is another of the powerful keys to recovery. Teens have the capacity to discover spirituality. Our teen needs access to a power that is higher and more powerful than him.

### Self-Worth (the Sunshine Principle)
Most high-risk and addicted teens have little or no self-esteem. The self-defeating beliefs, thoughts, and behaviors of addiction tear it down. Alcohol abuse may have led our teen to give up special talents, skills, and interests or to forfeit special opportunities or experiences that might have built her sense of self-worth. Abusing teens often cannot separate their real worth from the drug behavior. They see themselves as failures, losers, and worthless. Recovery puts our teen back on the road to self-discovery, and we can help by continuing to focus on the worth we see beneath the ugly mask of addiction.

Consider the sun. The sun is always emitting sunlight. But here on Earth days can be cloudy, rainy, cold, and dark because of clouds and atmospheric conditions. A teen's worth is like the sun: it always shines. But clouds of false beliefs, negative attitudes, dangerous emotions, self-defeating behaviors, and dangerous relationships block out the self-worth, casting shadows of doubt and regret and discouragement. Recovery, as well as life in general, will have its rainy days, but life doesn't have to be a self-made disaster.

### Positive Fun
To recover, our teen needs to have fun without the influence of alcohol, but the fun needs to be real or positive fun, not the illusion of a

thrill, a rush, or a high. We can help our teen identify and be involved in activities that bring positive fun. We should participate in having positive fun with our teen, and we can also help our teen link up with positive support groups that know how to have fun. Once our teen finds that he can have fun without alcohol, it will begin to reinforce his recovery.

### Real Happiness

Our teen needs a deeper happiness in life than fun can provide. By happiness, I mean a deeper sense of satisfaction, comfort, blessedness than mere pleasure or gratification of a physical need. Happiness comes from a sense of well-being, of deep satisfaction that our individual needs are being met and that we are a productive, contributing part of society. Joy and happiness do not come from fun, rather from activities that build self-esteem and feelings of kindness and love. Often when teens engage in a worthy service project for others or help an old person or do something kind for an animal, they find a deep satisfaction, a peace, and a serenity that they haven't felt before. When a teen can develop a talent or interest and receive some expression of appreciation or recognition for it, this brings happiness. A compliment, a sense of achievement, even doing something personal that brings satisfaction also bring happiness.

### Real Peace

Teens aren't interested much in serenity, but they do need to have an absence of grinding conflict in their lives. We should not expect our teens to always walk on eggshells, so to speak, by being model adults. We should anticipate vivid enthusiasm and impulsive activity that brings some bumping up against the fences of life. That is part of being a healthy adolescent. Nevertheless, behavior that is dangerous, self-destructive, and troublesome brings heavy conflict that is neither necessary nor desirable. Setting positive values, living by good standards, and avoiding conflicts with others bring peace. Just having alcohol out of a teen's life can bring peace, once the conflict between craving and sobriety lessens. We can help by preparing our family and home environment to minimize conflicts. It is important to realize that we don't have to be a perfect family or have a perfect atmosphere in our home all the time to be successful in helping our teen. Conflict and friction is natural and inherent in a family. After all, that is where the deepest living and feelings are had. When I speak of minimizing conflict in the home, I mean eliminating the big frustrations and inconsistencies, the negative influences that breed hopelessness and other extreme negative feelings.

### A Healthy Lifestyle

We can help our teen discover and implement a healthy lifestyle through our own example. We can help her practice daily behaviors that bring good health, and over time, these can become good habits. I can think of at least ten aspects of healthy living that are important to foster. The activities within each of these areas are many and fairly easily identified. They include physical health (eating, weight, appearance), spiritual health (prayer, meditating, reading, religious worship), leisure and recreation (sports, hobbies, talents, interests), intellectual health (education, learning, training), confidence and trust building (self, other people, Higher Power), family health, building a work ethic (chores, part-time job), social health (friends, peers, neighbors, and so on), gratitude building, and recovery maintenance. As parents, we can help our teen to set realistic goals in important health areas and to follow through.

### The Power to Act

Our teen cannot recover without making some important changes in the way she thinks, feels, and behaves. She has to change some relationships—with herself, with alcohol, with family, and with other people. Our family may also need to make important changes. We can help our teen access the power to make positive changes by our own example and encouragement.

### Stinking Thinking

Alcoholism is a disease of false beliefs, negative attitudes, and self-defeating self-talk. By self-talk I mean the messages we give ourselves. Alcoholic teens are fairly self-destructive and negative in their beliefs and thoughts. With the help of trained counselors, our teen can learn to send himself positive, helpful messages that promote sobriety. False beliefs and negative attitudes can be challenged and corrected. We can help by learning to give positive messages to our teen, also.

### Dangerous Emotions

Often alcoholic teens have strong emotions that they don't know how to resolve or cope with except through alcohol abuse. Our teen needs to learn to recognize, cope with, and resolve these dangerous emotions. Some of these feelings will undoubtedly be related to her relationship with us. We may also have strong feelings about our teen and what she's put us through. Working together to resolve these feelings by listening to each other and speaking honestly and openly about them will help. Strong feelings are not easily overcome. Our teen is responsible for her feelings and stress, but we can be sensitive to our role in those feelings and not get caught in blaming or finding fault. Resolution of some strong emotions, especially those that seem to be persistent and deep-seated, may well need the help of a professional counselor or even medication prescribed and monitored by a psychiatrist. Major depression is a frequent problem with teens.

*Self-Defeating Behavior*

Our teen may be used to doing what he wants and drinking when he feels stress or discomfort. He may be used to acting irresponsibly and without consideration for other people. He must change that behavior. He must learn to behave in society and to cope with stress or emotion without having to drink or be drunk. Behavior comes from inner beliefs and attitudes that generate thoughts and feelings. Behavior is managed by providing consequences for behavior and by teaching and instilling positive self-discipline. We should watch for and encourage growth in our teen's behavior through the following four stages, especially if our teen is in a treatment center and preparing to return home.

1. *Uncontrolled-unresponsive behavior:* Our teen does not seem to recognize bad or dangerous behavior and refuses to accept prompts from us or others. If our teen is exhibiting this type of behavior, he is at very high risk of relapse. If our teen is in treatment, this type of behavior is a sure sign that he is not ready to leave treatment and begin aftercare. We must be open with our teen about responsible behavior.

2. *Uncontrolled-responsive behavior:* Our teen seems not to recognize bad or dangerous behavior but generally responds positively to prompts from us or appropriate others. This means that our teen is not self-regulating but is willing to be regulated by others. This is, of course, better than the first behavior but certainly does not imply that she can sustain recovery on her own. She still needs to develop further values and skills and still needs heavy supervision and guidance.

3. *Partially controlled-responsive behavior:* Our teen controls some or much of his behavior and responds to positive prompts by a teen, a parent or other authority figure, or himself. When our

teen shows this type of self-regulation, we know that he is making positive gains. Values are starting to take and skills are strengthening. We should encourage and reward this type of behavior with trust, respect, and compliments. However, the teen is not ready, at this point, to shoulder full responsibility and independence.

4. *Controlled-responsive behavior:* Our teen requires little or no prompting in recognizing and avoiding bad or dangerous behavior. At this point, our teen is self-regulating and should be trusted to assume stewardship and control of her life and actions. Remember that all teenagers—even those who have not had a history of problem behavior—need continual supervision, monitoring, and discipline.

### Enabling and Dependent Relationships

Alcohol has been our teen's most important relationship, often to the exclusion of most others. Frequently, active sexual relationships have begun, not based on love or affection but related to alcohol. For our teen to lead a fulfilling life, alcohol must be replaced with other, meaningful relationships. The first relationship our teen must develop, which will be the most important, is his relationship with his own recovery. The recovery relationship must come before all other relationships, and all other relationships, including with family, must support that. Other extremely important relationships are with our teen's counselor, a sponsor from an AA group, and other professionals. Before our teen jumps back into relationships with others, it's crucial to ensure that his relationship with sobriety and his family support team is strong. Then make sure that all other relationships support recovery. A useful test for deciding if a relationship is useful and not dependent is to ask the following five questions:

- Does this relationship allow my teen to be honest and truthful?
- Does this relationship protect the health and life of my teen and family?
- Does this relationship support recovery and positive goals?
- Does this relationship prevent unnecessary trouble and destructive conflict?
- Does this relationship promote happiness and real satisfaction?

If we and our teen can answer yes to these questions, the relationship may well be a useful one. We should promote our teen's relationship with a sponsor from Alcoholics Anonymous, a professional counselor/therapist, and other positive adults and teens. As I said earlier, it is important that teens not feel isolated and alone in this quest for recovery. They need to know and feel that they are part of a system that is sharing and helping to lift the burdens with which they can identify. For this reason, peer groups managed at school or in a treatment setting are valuable. Some significant work is being done with the development of sobriety high schools. These schools are entirely populated by teens who have had serious problems with or addictions to alcohol or other drugs. They are remarkably integrated schools with healthy academics, extracurricular activities, and reinforcement for sobriety and recovery.

### The Power to Heal

Addiction causes wounds, emotional and physical, in our teen and in us, our family, and other important people. Recovery needs to promote the healing of these wounds. Healing may take a long time, depending upon the wound, but some level of healing is important to recovery from addiction. Many relapses occur because teens and parents and families failed to take the steps to truly heal. This is a spiritual exercise, not just a mental or physical one. It must go beyond simple expressions of "I'm sorry" and "it's okay." We cannot simply sweep the pain and trauma of living with addiction under the rug. It must be dealt with. Healing is blocked by pride and by people who refuse to forgive or make amends. If our teen has no sense of remorse for what she's done to others, she may need long-term help. But most teens have feelings that come out when they are thawed by recovery. We and our teen need to have at least two important things happen to stimulate real healing: forgiveness and making amends.

### The Miracle of Forgiveness

Most likely, parent and child have hurt each other. Alcoholism always wounds. After recognizing the things we have done, we need to seek forgiveness for them from our teen. As we exercise humility, it will soften the heart of our own grieving child. Heartfelt forgiveness is a miracle because of its healing power. We can forgive the harmful things our teen has done to us, whether he asks for it or not. Forgiveness is a cleansing, lightening process that strengthens us. Holding grudges and feeling vengeful are darkening, suffocating behaviors. True forgiveness softens the heart, opens the spirit, and heals wounds. If our teen has a difficult time forgiving us, try forgiving him first. If he experiences our forgiveness, perhaps he will be more able to forgive us. That said, we must remember that true forgiveness and true healing through forgiveness cannot be forced or mandated. It must come genuinely from a broken heart and a contrite spirit.

### Making Amends

We shouldn't be too quick to absolve our teen of all the trouble she has caused and the damage she has inflicted. At the same time, we need to be reasonable and kind in our approach. Making amends means restoring damage. It is a physical activity that is crucial to healing. If restitution is not part of the equation, it is weak medicine. We can help our teen make amends, without holding grudges or using this process as a means of punishing or getting even. While we forgive, we also recognize that holding our teen accountable for her behaviors will make a more responsible person out of her.

### The Power to Sustain Recovery

Recovery from alcoholism requires complete abstinence from alcohol. This is the first and greatest commandment: *Thou shalt not drink.* And the second is *Thou shalt fill thy life with positive replacements.* Recovery that is focused entirely on abstinence and nothing else is doomed. Our teen must find reasons to stay sober. He needs to find satisfaction, happiness, self-esteem, and success. This is accomplished through effective planning, making commitments, and thorough execution of a plan. Parents and other family members become particularly vital in this role.

#### Profile of a Relapse

Relapse is predictable and preventable. Teens relapse for a few specific reasons. (1) They fail to see recovery as a way of life; rather, they think it is just an activity that they must do for a short time and then they can return to old behaviors and relationships. (2) They become fixated on not drinking and fail to find meaning, success, and happiness in their lives. (3) They don't have a plan or commitment to their plan. (4) They don't have a support team that is loyal to their sobriety. (5) They fail to implement the plan and stick with it.

It is crucial that we, as parents, understand our teen's personal warning signs of potential relapse and that we have an emergency plan prepared to put into action. Relapse to drinking usually happens in the mind before it happens in reality: *thinking and feeling precede the drinking.* We should look for the warning signs in our teen's thinking (which includes beliefs and attitudes), coping with emotions, impulsive and self-defeating behavior, and relationships with others. If we are observant, we can see it coming and help head it off. Here are some key signals to look for:

- His beliefs and attitudes and self-talk turn negative, hopeless, or discouraged.
- His lifestyle begins to collapse; he doesn't thrive or fit in; he is bored.
- He rushes to get his plan over with and return to the way things were.
- He has difficulty managing stress, anger, discouragement, and other emotions.
- He becomes impulsive and fails to follow his plan for happiness.
- He begins to withdraw and isolate himself from family and others.
- He begins to engage in past patterns of troublesome behavior.
- He returns to his using lifestyle: in dressing, grooming, sleeping, eating, and so on.
- He begins associating with old using friends.
- He returns to places where he used to drink.
- He stops communicating with us and becomes sullen and withdrawn.

### Planning for Success

Recovery does not just happen. It must be planned for and executed. It works best when it is a team effort, not just left to our teen. A major danger is the tendency for teen, parents, and family to say, "Well, we've solved that problem. Now we can return to a normal life and get on with what is really important." There is no such thing as "a normal life" after recovery. That is to say, we cannot return to life as we knew it. It was that kind of life that brought this problem on in the first place. We must practice new and better ways of living and dealing with things. It is our privilege to help our teen and other family members put together a plan for continuing recovery. If our teen is in a treatment program and preparing to come home, the plan should be made and discussed prior to leaving the program.

I believe, from my experiences, that two plans are important: a plan for continuing recovery once initial treatment is completed and a personal emergency relapse prevention plan for emergencies. Parents should be involved in both of these plans. Let's look at the difference and what these plans should include.

- *The Recovery Plan:* While she is still in active treatment—residential or outpatient—our child should make a plan for how to sustain sobriety and recovery. Parents and family members should also write a family plan on how they can support the teen and manage the family so that it does not relapse into old problem patterns. These plans should be integrated and shared between our family and our teen in treatment so that everyone understands them and so that they complement each other. These plans should include a mission statement and commitment to sobriety and recovery, meaningful and age-appropriate goals, and statements of actions to accomplish these goals. They should include a plan of support that contains seven key activities (professional counseling, self-help groups such as AA, proper diet, regular exercise, stress management, spiritual development, and communication—with self through meditation, with other family members through family time and councils, and with a Higher Power through prayer). The plan should also identify key people on the support team, including parents, siblings, perhaps relatives, positive friends and peers, and other involved adults. Only people loyal to recovery can be members of the team. The plan also needs to outline realistic time management; the pursuit of interests, hobbies, and talents; and limits on friendships and peer relationships. It must be remembered that the first relationship of a recovering teen must be with his recovery. All other relationships must support that end.

- *The Personal Emergency Relapse Prevention Plan:* The personal emergency relapse prevention plan (PERPP) can take any form, but it is best to keep it simple. It should be prepared by our teen but shared and discussed with family members and others on the support team so that they can support the plan. The PERPP should contain at least the following information: names and telephone numbers of people who can help in case of emergency; places (addresses and locations) to go for help, such as sponsor, counselor, or clean friend; actions to take upon sensing the emergency, such as to call a sponsor, get away from the temptation, say a prayer, or call a team member; actions to take if the teen slips and uses again (these actions need to promote honesty, admission, and positive action); and some thoughts or sayings that will motivate the teen in a moment of crisis. These thoughts can come from meditation books, AA or Twelve Step slogans, religious scripture, or other places. Quotes such as "Think! Think! Think!" or "Easy does it" or "First things first" are easy, helpful reminders to focus. This plan can be posted on the refrigerator or some conspicuous place, and the recovering teen can carry a copy with him.

## Building Bridges

Our teen has likely burned most of her bridges with other people because of addictive behavior. Love and trust with family members is perhaps in ashes. Reputations with schoolteachers, administrators, schoolmates, neighbors, sober peers, police, community proprietors, and others have probably smoldered in the aftermath of her behavior. Our teen will need help in building new bridges across the past to a happier, more successful future. She'll need us to be her advocate, mentor, and champion. Failure to rebuild will result in renewed discouragement and high risk for relapse. Our teen needs to understand that Rome was not built in a day or by one action; neither will reputations be rebuilt in a moment or by a single act. We can help our teen stay focused on sobriety and on following her plan, instead of worrying whether people trust her. Trust from others will come in due time as a by-product of her efforts. Our teen will also need to burn some old bridges, with people, places, and things that enable and encourage relapse.

## Conclusion: The Power of Spirituality

If we humans are nothing more than a lump of flesh, a creation of biological mitosis and meiosis, as some believe, then I'm not sure that there would be much purpose in worrying about addiction and recovery, for life would have no meaningful purpose or hope. We would be but a spark jettisoned into the black night, to burn momentarily then forever disappear. Most of us hope for something more that will lend an extended purpose to what we do in our lives.

There are those who say that teens are not cognitively developed enough to grasp intangible concepts such as spirituality, and therefore it has no value for them. There are those who discredit the role and importance of spirituality in recovery and healthy living. I believe that we do our teens and ourselves a disservice in disavowing the spiritual side of our nature, and we certainly dilute the power of recovery by so doing. My experience as an addictions counselor, a therapist of teens, and a parent has proved to me time and again the awesome power that comes when someone in recovery rises above or, perhaps better said, goes beyond her physical nature and taps her spiritual capacities.

What is spirituality and what is its role in recovery? Is it merely religion or being a member of a religious denomination? For me, spirituality is much more than that. Spirituality is a consciousness that life is more than physical, that it has a much deeper, grander side, a side that cannot be seen by normal physical senses, a side that I must find by other means. The spiritual side of us is tender, kind, loving, and wholesome. The physical, or "natural," person is filled with egotistical cravings, appetites, and tangible needs. These two dimensions, when brought into harmony so that they complement each other and when brought into harmony with a higher and universal source of spirituality, bring an inner peace and joy that no physical pleasure can replicate. This is especially true when the spiritual dimension brings the more base physical cravings under control. I call this state of congruency spirituality.

Recovery is not purely a physical overcoming, a grappling with physical cravings, but involves a deeper, inner evolving, a spiritual grappling with self and purpose, an inner empowerment. True, a teen can overcome the craving of his body by denying it alcohol, but abstinence alone leaves him but an empty shell. The attributes of his soul that inspire self-worth, hope, trust, and true joy are not physical but spiritual in nature and must be accessed through the spirit. Recovery is a spiritual filling of the soul that brings true joy and satisfaction and comfort. Indeed, recovery is the discovery of the spiritual nature above the physical and allowing that spiritual part to exercise dominion over the natural or physical part of us.

Alcoholism begins as a disease of the physical body called dependence, but it quickly evolves into a spiritual disease of addiction. If allowed to persist, alcoholism will strip a teen of her moral values and human decency; it will take away that special light that glows within her, turning her vulgar, dark, and hollow.

Thus, recovery requires tapping into a spiritual source, accessing power that is higher and more powerful than our own. Recovery is the recognition of that possibility, of the spiritual conscience, and a teen is perfectly positioned for such a recognition. I think that teens are less encumbered by life's biases and lack of faith than are adults, and I think they have the capacity to tune in to spiritual matters if guided. Spirituality is real, and it is an essential ally in our quest for recovery. Teens need spirituality in their lives and in their recovery, and they are capable of receiving it if we adults stop holding them back with our nay-saying and lack of faith.

Spirituality in recovery exists on at least three levels. A teen's growth in spiritual awareness must begin at the level that he is able to grasp. The first level is individual spiritual awareness. It is a personal congruency between the inner feelings and workings of the spirit and the outer behaviors of the body. This is significant for teens because they are seeking to discover who they really are. It's best to discover both inner and outer and bring them into harmony. Unity lessens conflict and stress. As a teen becomes more aware of his inner spirit and listens to its promptings, he will find an ability to be more peaceable and kind and wholesome because the spirit is like that. He will see himself as more than a physical being, and he will find strength to exercise appropriate control of his physical body. This produces self-esteem and love of self.

The second level of spirituality is social spirituality, or a unity or congruency between self and other people. This level of spirituality causes teens to realize that they are part of something larger and more complex and that they can learn to harness their own appetites, behaviors, and wants to the benefit of the larger whole, for a greater purpose. When they are capable of this type of spirituality, they are capable of giving and receiving true love.

The ultimate level of spirituality is to bring ourselves as individuals into harmony with a Higher Power. The more accurately we are able to discover and experience the true nature of this Higher Power in our lives, the stronger is its influence upon us. As teens discover who their Higher Power is through their own spiritual quest, they will realize that they can trust and love this power and that it will raise them to a higher, more powerful level of living, something alcohol and alcoholic relationships never could do. They can live without fear or intimidation in a physical world because of their spiritual insights. They can see beyond trying moments with greater hope and peace.

I hosted an online chat room for Hazelden one evening and met a lady from Ireland. We began chatting about the role God plays in recovery, and she noted that it had taken her years of pain and addiction before she realized that God was not a vindictive, unforgiving being, as she had been taught, but someone who loved her unconditionally and wanted her to succeed. When she cast out her limiting beliefs and opened herself up to new spiritual perspectives, she was freed to accept her Higher Power on a level that lifted her and helped her become free to recover. That is the power of faith.

# Notes

## Chapter 1: Perspectives on Alcohol

1. U.S. Department of Health and Human Services, Substance Abuse and Mental Health Services Administration, Office of Applied Studies, *1998 National Household Survey on Drug Abuse*. Available online at www.samhsa.gov/oas/nhsda.htm.

2. L. D. Johnston, P. M. O'Malley, and J. G. Bachman, "Drug Trends in 1999 among American Teens Are Mixed," University of Michigan News and Information Services press release, 17 December 1999. Available online at www.monitoringthefuture.org/pressreleases/99drugpr.html.

3. U.S. Department of Health and Human Services, Substance Abuse and Mental Health Services Administration, Office of Applied Studies, *1999 National Household Survey on Drug Abuse*. Available online at www.samhsa.gov/oas/nhsda.htm.

4. L. D. Johnston, P. M. O'Malley, and J. G. Bachman, *Monitoring the Future National Results on Adolescent Drug Use: Overview of Key Findings, 2002* (Bethesda, Md.: National Institute on Drug Abuse, 2003). Available at www.alcoholfreechildren.org/gs/pubs/html/stat.htm.

5. A. C. Wagenaar, T. L. Toomey, and D. M. Murray, "Sources of Alcohol for Underage Drinkers," *Journal of Studies on Alcohol* 57, no. 3 (1996): 325–33. Available at www.alcoholfreechildren.org/gs/pubs/html/stat.htm.

6. J. A. Grunbaum, L. Kann, S. A. Kinchen, B. Williams, J. G. Ross, R. Lowry, and L. Kolbe, "Youth Risk Behavior Surveillance—United States, 2001," *MMWR Surveillance Summaries* 51, SS04 (28 June 2002): 1–64. Available online at www.cdc.gov/mmwr/preview/mmwrhtml/ss5104a1.htm and at www.alcoholfreechildren.org/gs/pubs/html/stat.htm.

7. Adams Business Research, *Adams Liquor Handbook 2001*, *Adams Wine Handbook 2001*, and *Adams Beer Handbook 2001* (New York: Adams Business Media, 2001). N. Blisard et al., "Analyses of Generic Dairy Advertising, 1984–97," technical bulletin no. 1873 (Washington, D.C.: U.S. Department of Agriculture, Food and Rural Economics Division, Economic

Research Service, 1999). Available at www.alcoholfreechildren.org/gs/pubs/html/stat.htm.

8. J. W. Grube and L. Wallack, "Television Beer Advertising and Drinking Knowledge, Beliefs, and Intentions among Schoolchildren," *American Journal of Public Health* 84, no. 2 (1994): 254–59. Available at www.alcoholfreechildren.org/gs/pubs/html/stat.htm.

9. B. F. Grant, "Estimates of U.S. Children Exposed to Alcohol Abuse and Dependence in the Family," *American Journal of Public Health* 90, no. 1 (2000): 112–15. Available at www.alcoholfreechildren.org/gs/pubs/html/stat.htm.

10. The Weekly Reader, *National Survey on Drugs and Alcohol* (Middletown, Conn.: Field Publications, 1995). Available at www.alcoholfreechildren.org/gs/pubs/html/stat.htm.

11. J. D. Hawkins et al., "Exploring the Effects of Age of Alcohol Use Initiation and Psychosocial Risk Factors on Subsequent Alcohol Misuse," *Journal of Studies on Alcohol* 58, no. 3 (1997): 280–90. Available at www.alcoholfreechildren.org/gs/pubs/html/stat.htm.

12. Johnston, O'Malley, and Bachman, "Drug Trends in 1999 among American Teens Are Mixed."

13. B. F. Grant, T. C. Harford, D. A. Dawson, P. Chou, M. Dufour, and R. Pickering, "Prevalence of DSM-IV Alcohol Abuse and Dependence, United States, 1992," *Alcohol Health and Research World* 18, no. 3 (1994): 243–48. Available at www.alcoholfreechildren.org/gs/pubs/html/stat.htm.

**Chapter 2: Alcohol and the Body**

1. S. A. Brown et al., "Neurocognitive Functioning of Adolescents: Effects of Protracted Alcohol Use," *Alcoholism: Clinical and Experimental Research* 2, no. 2 (2000): 164–71. Available at www.alcoholfreechildren.org/gs/pubs/html/stat.htm.

2. U.S. Department of Health and Human Services, Substance Abuse and Mental Health Services Administration, *The Relationship between Mental Health and Substance Abuse among Adolescents* (Rockville, Md.: Substance Abuse and Mental Health Services Administration, 1999). Available at www.alcoholfreechildren.org/gs/pubs/html/stat.htm.

3. E. Z. Hanna, Y. Hsaio-Ye, and M. Dufour, "The Relationship of Drinking Alone and Other Substance Use Alone and in Combination to Health and Behavior Problems among Youth Aged 12–16: Findings from the Third National Health and Nutrition Survey (NHANES III)," paper pre-

sented at the 23d Annual Scientific Meeting of the Research Society on Alcoholism, 24–29 June 2000, Denver, Colo. Available at www.alcohol freechildren.org/gs/pubs/html/stat.htm.

4. U.S. Department of Health and Human Services, National Institutes of Health, National Institute on Alcohol Abuse and Alcoholism, "State Trends in Alcohol Problems, 1979–1992," *U.S. Alcohol Epidemiologic Data Reference Manual,* vol. 5 (Rockville, Md.: National Institute on Alcohol Abuse and Alcoholism, 1996). Available at www.alcoholfreechildren.org/gs/pubs/html/stat.htm.

5. Hanna et al., "Drinking, Smoking and Blood Pressure: Do Their Relationships among Youth Foreshadow What We Know among Adults?" paper presented at the American Public Health Association Annual Meeting, November 1999, Chicago, Ill. Available at www.alcoholfree children.org/gs/pubs/html/stat.htm.

6. C. A. Martin, A. G. Mainous, and T. Curry, "Alcohol Use in Adolescent Females: Correlates of Estradiol and Testosterone," *American Journal on Addiction* 8, no. 1 (1999): 9–14. Available at www.alcohol freechildren.org/gs/pubs/html/stat.htm.

7. Ibid.

8. C. S. Lieber, "Alcohol and Hepatitis C," *Alcohol Research and Health* 25, no. 4 (2001): 245–54.

9. D. J. Meyerhoff, "Effects of Alcohol and HIV Infection on the Central Nervous System," *Alcohol Research and Health* 25, no. 4 (2001): 288–98.

10. V. Bagnardi, M. Blangiardo, C. La Vecchia, and G. Corrao, "Alcohol Consumption and the Risk of Cancer: A Meta-Analysis," *Alcohol Research and Health* 25, no. 4 (2001): 263–70.

11. Ibid.

12. J. R. Hankin, "Fetal Alcohol Syndrome Prevention Research," *Alcohol Research and Health* 26, no. 1 (2002): 58–65.

13. R. T. Turner and J. D. Sibonga, "Effects of Alcohol Use and Estrogen on Bone," *Alcohol Research and Health* 25, no. 4 (2001): 276–81.

14. J. M. McGinnis and W. H. Foege, "Actual Causes of Death in the United States," *Journal of the American Medical Association* 270, no. 18 (1993): 2207–212. Available at www.alcoholfreechildren.org/gs/pubs/html/stat.htm.

15. U.S. Department of Health and Human Services, National Institutes of Health, National Institute on Alcohol Abuse and Alcoholism,

"Drinking in the United States: Main Findings from the 1992 National Longitudinal Alcohol Epidemiologic Survey (NLAES)," *US Alcohol Epidemiologic Data Reference Manual,* vol. 6 (Rockville, Md.: National Institute on Alcohol Abuse and Alcoholism, 1998). Available at www.alcoholfreechildren.org/gs/pubs/html/stat.htm.

16. W. L. Dees, V. K. Srivastava, and J. K. Hiney, "Alcohol and Female Puberty: The Role of Intraovarian Systems," *Alcohol Research and Health* 25, no. 4 (2001): 271–75.

17. M. A. Emanuele and N. Emanuele, "Alcohol and the Male Reproductive System," *Alcohol Research and Health* 25, no. 4 (2001): 282–87.

18. L. A. Greenfeld and M. A. Henneberg, "Victim and Offender Self-Reports of Alcohol Involvement in Crime," *Alcohol Research and Health* 25, no. 1 (2001): 20–31.

19. A. Abbey, T. Zawacki, P. O. Buck, A. M. Clinton, and P. McAuslan, "Alcohol and Sexual Assault," *Alcohol Research and Health* 25, no. 1 (2001): 43–51.

20. R. Hingson, T. Heeren, and M. Winter, "Lower Legal Blood Alcohol Limits for Young Drivers," *Public Health Reports* 109, no. 6 (1994): 738–44. Available at www.alcoholfreechildren.org/gs/pubs/html/stat.htm.

21. Grunbaum et al., "Youth Risk Behavior Surveillance—United States, 2001."

22. S. G. Tibbets and J. N. Whittemore, "The Interactive Effects of Low Self-Control and Commitment to School on Substance Abuse among College Students," *Psychological Reports* 90, no. 1 (February 2002): 327–37.

23. Turner and Sibonga, "Effects of Alcohol Use and Estrogen on Bone."

24. K. J. Mukamal and E. B. Rimm, "Alcohol's Effects on the Risk for Coronary Heart Disease," *Alcohol Research and Health* 25, no. 4 (2001): 255–62.

25. M. A. Sayette, "Does Drinking Reduce Stress?" *Alcohol Research and Health* 23, no. 4 (1999): 250–55.

**Chapter 3: Adolescence and Alcohol**

1. Leadership to Keep Children Alcohol Free, *Keep Kids Alcohol Free: Strategies for Action.* Available online at www.alcoholfreechildren.org/gs/pubs/html/prev.htm.

2. The Weekly Reader, *National Survey on Drugs and Alcohol.*

3. Stephen R. Covey, *Spiritual Roots of Human Relations* (Salt Lake City, Utah: Deseret Books, 1988), 142–48.

4. B. F. Grant and D. A. Dawson, "Age at Onset of Alcohol Use and Its Association with DSM-IV Alcohol Abuse and Dependence: Results from the National Longitudinal Alcohol Epidemiologic Survey," *Journal of Substance Abuse* 9 (1997): 103–10. Available at www.alcoholfreechildren. org/gs/pubs/html/stat.htm.

### Chapter 4: Alcohol Addiction

1. Greenfeld and Henneberg, "Victim and Offender Self-Reports of Alcohol Involvement in Crime."

2. Pacific Institute for Research and Evaluation, *Costs of Underage Drinking*, prepared 5 September 2002. Available at www.alcoholfree children.org/gs/pubs/html/stat.htm.

3. H. Harwood, D. Fountain, and G. Livermore, *The Economic Costs of Alcohol and Drug Abuse in the United States, 1992* (Rockville, Md.: National Institute on Drug Abuse, 1998). Available at www.alcoholfreechildren.org/ gs/pubs/html/stat.htm.

4. Emanuele and Emanuele, "Alcohol and the Male Reproductive System."

5. Dees, Srivastava, and Hiney, "Alcohol and Female Puberty: The Role of Intraovarian Systems."

6. Used with permission of Bonner Ritchie.

### Chapter 7: Prevention and Diversion

1. Grant and Dawson, "Age at Onset of Alcohol Use and Its Association with DSM-IV Alcohol Abuse and Dependence: Results from the National Longitudinal Alcohol Epidemiologic Survey."

2. Leadership to Keep Children Alcohol Free, *Keep Kids Alcohol Free: Strategies for Action*. Available online at www.alcoholfreechildren.org/gs/ pubs/html/prev.htm. See also K. A. Komro and T. L. Toomey, "Strategies to Prevent Underage Drinking," *Alcohol Research and Health* 26, no. 1 (2002): 5–14.

3. L. B. Nissen, *Alternate Routes: An Alcohol Diversion Program*, facilitator's guide (Center City, Minn.: Hazelden, 2002), ix–x.

# Index

abstinence, 14–15, 59–63, 135,
    157–58, 192, 195, 214
academic achievement. *See* school
    performance
acamprosate, 14
acceptance, 66–67, 102–3, 187
    of help, 110, 200, 201–2
accidents, car, 39
addiction. *See* alcoholism
adolescence. *See* teenagers
*Adolescent Recovery Plan*, 89
advertisements, 13, 16, 17, 149
aftercare, 185, 191, 216–17
alcohol
    availability of, 16, 67
    benefits of, 40
    chemical composition of, 22
    craving for, 82, 83, 84, 94, 107, 195
    as depressant, 25, 26–27, 28–29
    as gateway drug, 82
    healthy attitude on, 9
    historical perspective on, 10–13
    in the media, 13, 17, 149
    medicinal use of, 11
    as most widely used drug, 13, 16
    preoccupation with, 82
    tolerance of, 80–81
alcohol abuse, 6, 77–80, 85
    *See also* intervention; prevention

consequences of, 73–74, 80
criteria for, 78–80
denial of, 85, 156–57
family problems and, 78, 138–39
health risks with, 34–37
lack of knowledge about, 74–75
lifestyle of, 45, 81, 158–59
rewards for, 74
Alcoholics Anonymous, 109, 186–87
alcoholism, 6, 14, 77, 80–98, 209
    accurate information on, 202
    amoral behavior due to, 86, 93, 94
    causes of, 82–83
    consequences of, 73–74, 81,
      116–17, 129–30
    cost of, 113–20
    cure for, 167–68
    demands of, 53, 66–67, 75
    as disease, 80, 84, 86–87, 95–96
    as disease of attitudes, 108–9
    as disease of denial, 111, 200
    as disease of refusals, 109–11, 132
    lack of control with, 80, 81, 112
    as lifelong condition, 86–87, 167,
      195, 196
    maintenance, 87
    potential for, 21, 32
    prevalence of, 19, 99
    prevention of. *See* prevention

229

progression of, 82, 84–86
symptoms of, 80–82
treatment for. *See* treatment
in the workforce, 88
alcohol use, 6
abstaining from, 59–63
age of onset for, 73, 84, 135
among teenagers, 13, 16, 19
attitudes promoting, 70–71
brain functions and, 25, 26, 29, 39,
157
community response to, 50, 61,
88–89, 105, 149–50
crime and, 87–88, 93–94, 118
deaths from, 28, 32, 37, 87, 88
developmental tasks and, 21, 27,
37–38, 89–92, 196–99
double standard on, 70–71
environment factors in, 70–72, 83
experimentation phase of, 84–85, 93
laws governing, 12, 72, 77, 166
national cost of, 88
national decrease in, 13
by parents, 8–9, 67, 138, 145, 159
parents' perspectives on, 5, 6–8
personal reasons for, 63–66, 75
physical effects of, 25, 26–27, 29,
30, 31–32
risks of, 33–40
short-term danger of, 21, 27
as social problem, 11–12, 13–14
social reasons for, 66–70
societal acceptance of, 12–13, 17,
40–41
teens' financing of, 79, 86, 115–16
teens' perspectives on, 16–20
*Alternate Routes*, 152–53
American Psychiatric Association, 78,
80
anger, 64, 65
Antabuse, 180
assertiveness skills, 67, 68

assessment services, 172–74
attitudes, 108–11

beer bonging, 28, 88
binge drinking, 13, 16, 19, 28, 40, 166
blaming, 156, 201
blood alcohol content, 12, 39
bootlegging, 12
boredom, 63–64, 147
boys, 16, 38
brain functions, 14, 22, 27, 74–75
central nervous system and, 25, 26,
157
effects of alcohol on, 29, 39
pathways to, 28
psychoactive drugs and, 24, 25
serotonin and, 29
breast cancer, 35
Burkhe, Anne, 132

cancer, 35, 36, 168
central nervous system (CNS), 25–27
effects of alcohol on, 28–32, 39
psychoactive drugs and, 22–25
receptor sites in, 30, 31
character flaws, 93
chemicals, 22, 27
gaba as, 29
neurotransmitters as, 23, 25, 27
child abuse, 106
codependent relationships, 90–91
cognitive growth, 90, 197
communication, 7, 8, 91
clear, 136–40, 144–45, 146
during interventions, 160–63
respectful, 136–38
community environments, 50, 61,
88–89, 105, 149–50
control, loss of, 80, 81, 112
co-occurring disorders, 95, 179, 181,
182, 183
counseling, 180, 183, 184, 191, 209

Covey, Stephen R., 69–70, 133
cravings, 82, 83, 84, 94, 107, 195
crime, 87–88, 93–94, 118
crisis management care, 180
curiosity, 64, 93

DARE (Drug Abuse Resistance
    Education), 14
day-care treatment, 181
denial, 85, 109–10, 111, 120, 156–57
    during interventions, 161, 162,
        163–64
    of parents, 156–57
depressants, 25, 26–27, 32
depression, 34, 209
despair, 129–30
detoxification, 158, 179
developmental tasks, 21, 27, 37–38,
    89–92, 196–99
diabetes, 169
disulfiram, 180
diversion programs, 150–53
dopamine, 29–31
driving under the influence, 12, 39,
    78–79, 87, 88
drug prevention programs, 13–14
dual disorders (co-occurring), 95, 179,
    181, 182, 183

Eighteenth Amendment, 12
emergency help, 165
emotional growth, 90–91, 197, 210–11
emotional pain, 100–8, 117–18,
    124–25, 209
estradiol, 35
estrogen levels, 40
ethanol, 22
extracurricular activities, 147, 148

faith, 119, 132, 197, 211
family councils, 125
family counseling, 184

family pledges, 144
family relationships, 78, 115–16,
    138–39, 143
    See also parents
    support given by, 155, 177, 182,
        188–91, 203–4, 207–8, 216–17
fetal alcohol syndrome (FAS), 17, 37
financial costs, of alcohol abuse, 119–20
flashbacks, 24
forgiveness, 120, 213

gaba, 29
genetics, 14, 82–83, 106–7, 138–39,
    167–68
girls/women, 11, 16, 34, 35, 40
God, 118–19, 197, 221
group counseling, 183

hallucinogens, 23–24
happiness, 207
Hazelden, 170
health risks, 34–37
hepatitis C virus, 36
heroin, 30
high blood pressure, 35
Higher Power, 118–19, 131, 132, 184,
    198, 199, 205–6, 221
Hinckley, Gordon B., 69
HIV/AIDS, 35, 36
honesty, 162, 187, 200–1
hopelessness, 82, 87, 88, 102, 202–3
huffing, 24
humility, 199, 200

inhalants, 24
intervention, 155–66
    action plan in, 163
    change of residence as, 158
    methods useful for, 160–63
    parental control following, 163,
        164–65
    parental responsibility for, 155–56

police involvement in, 166
support during, 160, 165
timing of, 159–60, 163–64
"I" statements, 137

learning disabilities, 49, 105–6
legal problems, 38, 79, 118, 145, 166
leisure activities, 183
life skills, 91–92, 208
liver disease, 36

making amends, 213–14
marijuana, 16
marriage counseling, 184
Maxwell, Neil A., 5
media influences, 13, 16, 17, 149
medical care, 166, 184–84
medications, 39, 179–80, 181–82, 209
meditation, 184
Melville, Herman, 131
memory loss, 33–34
methamphetamine, 31, 83

naltrexone, 14, 180
narcotics, 10
National Coalition of Governors'
    Spouses, 143
National Institute of Alcohol Abuse
    and Addictions (NIAAA), 54
National Longitudinal Alcohol
    Epidemiological Survey, 13
neglect, of children, 106
nervous system. See central nervous
    system (CNS)
neurotransmitters, 23, 25, 27, 29–31
Newsweek, 93
Nissen, Laura Burney, 152
nonconformity, 71

osteoporosis, 37, 40
outpatient care, 180–81
overdoses, 166

Pacific Institute for Research and
    Evaluation, 88
parents, 5, 6–8
    alcohol use of, 8–9, 67, 138, 145,
        159
    control exercised by, 163, 164–65
    denial of, 156–57
    honest communication of, 7, 8
    inspiring teens, 130
    making changes in their lives, 9–10
    permissiveness of, 69
    in recovery, 139
    as supervisors, 68
peace, 207–8
peer influences, 18, 66, 67, 69
peer programs, 147
physical development, 90, 104, 196–97
powerlessness, 192, 199
pregnancies, 35, 37
prevention, 135–50
    abstinence as, 135, 138, 139
    clear communication in, 136–40,
        144–45, 146
    consequences for drinking in, 139
    education in, 143
    family pledges in, 144
    parental involvement with teens as,
        145–46, 147, 148
    promoting protection factors in,
        140–41
    reducing risk of drinking in, 140–41
    of relapse, 185–86, 217, 218
    teamwork required in, 135–36,
        142–43, 148–49, 160
professional help, 74, 104, 156–57, 165
    for assessments, 172–74
    refusing to get, 110, 132, 167
prohibition, 12
psychedelic drugs, 23–24
psychiatrists, 181–82, 209
psychoactive drugs, 22–25, 26, 27

psychological problems, 34, 94–95, 104, 111–12, 165, 173
puberty, 37–38, 48, 90

rationalizations, 159
rebellion, 64–65, 69, 71
recovery, 14–15, 128, 192–93, 195–96, 211
  See also spirituality
  counseling during, 183, 184, 191
  difficulty of, 112–13, 131, 132, 165, 195, 199, 203
  family support during, 188–89, 191, 203–4, 207–8
  filling voids during, 196, 206–7, 214
  forgiveness and, 120, 213
  healthy lifestyle in, 208
  medication during, 179–80
  meditation and, 184
  moral values and, 173–74
  parents in, 139
  planning successful, 215–16
  as process of becoming, 192–93
  reasons for pursuing, 128–34, 192–93, 195, 206–8
  reestablishing trust during, 204–6
  resources to assist, 169–71
  social relationships during, 173, 211–12, 217–18
  support systems during, 186–88, 192, 212, 216–17
  as time of healing, 212–14
recreation, 183
refusal skills, 67–68
relapse, 168, 185
  prevention of, 185–86, 217, 218
  reasons for, 109, 186, 191, 212–13, 214
  signs of, 214–15
reproductive problems, 38, 90
resentment, 64–65
residential treatment, 182

ReVia, 180
Richards, Bob, 130
role models, 51–52, 75, 104

school performance, 37, 61, 78, 91–92, 105–6, 114–15
  during treatment, 173, 185
school programs, 148–49, 181
self-confidence, 103, 146–47
self-discipline, 146, 210
self-discovery, 129–30, 206
self-empowerment, 131, 153, 199
self-esteem, 48–49, 56, 62, 68, 105, 207
self-regulation, 210–11
self-talk, 108, 209
self-worth, 56, 103, 129, 206
serotonin, 29
sexual assault, 38–39, 91
sexual behavior, 48, 91, 116
sexually transmitted diseases, 35
sobriety high schools, 212
social growth, 90–91, 197–98, 210–11
socioeconomic status, 72, 105
spirituality, 62, 118–19, 198, 205–6, 218–21
sponsors, 187–88
stimulants, 23
stinking thinking, 108–9, 209
Strategies to Prevent Underage Drinking (NIAAA), 54
stress, 34, 40, 65
suicides, 34, 88
support systems, 186–88, 192, 212, 216–17

teenagers, 6, 7, 15–20, 32–33
  abstaining from alcohol, 59–63
  cognitive growth of, 90, 197
  cultural influences on, 52–54
  developmental tasks of, 21, 27, 37–38, 89–92, 196–99

emotional growth of, 90–91, 197, 210–11
emotional pain of, 100–8, 117–18, 124–25, 209
emotional volatility of, 44–45, 49
familial influence on, 17–18, 51, 60–62, 78, 138–39
peer influence on, 18, 66, 67, 69
physical challenges of, 46–47, 48, 65
physical development of, 90, 104, 196–97
psychological challenges of, 48–50, 58–59, 65–66
rates of alcohol use among, 13, 16, 19
at risk, 16, 17–18, 53, 54–59, 94, 95
role models of, 51–52, 74, 104
seeking independence, 44–45, 65, 71
sexual behavior of, 48, 91, 116
social growth of, 50–51, 90–91, 197–98, 210–11
transition period of, 43–44, 112
temperance movements, 11–12
testosterone, 35, 38
Thoreau, Henry David, 130
tobacco, 16, 36, 37, 168
treatment, 19–20, 164, 167–93
aftercare plans in, 185, 191, 216–17
approaches to, 176, 177, 178, 180–81
assessment services and, 172–74
belief systems and, 177–78
changing programs during, 176
choosing appropriate, 171–72, 175–79, 180–81, 182
components of, 179, 181–82, 183, 185, 186
cooperating with, 174–75
crisis care as, 180
day-care, 181
detoxification in, 179
educational programs during, 173, 181, 185
effectiveness of, 14–15
family support during, 155, 177, 182, 188–91, 216–17
goals of, 96, 158, 179, 201–2
key relationships in, 189–91
outpatient care as, 180–81
psychiatric care during, 181–82
relapse prevention strategies in, 186
residential, 182
staff members, 190–91
unsuccessful, 168–69
trust, 204–6, 218
Twelve Step programs, 178, 205

U.S. Department of Agriculture, 13

violence, 38–39

willpower, 93, 157
wine, 10–11
withdrawal, 81, 85–86, 117
women/girls, 11, 16, 34, 35, 40

"You" statements, 137

# About the Author

Stephen Biddulph holds a master's degree in counseling psychology. He has been a family, marriage, and child counselor for the military Family Service Centers and a supervising therapist and director of adolescent substance and addictions treatment at Provo Canyon School. He is the author of *The Adolescent Recovery Plan: A Curriculum of Recovery* and *Continuing Care: A Team Approach*, both published by Hazelden Foundation.

He was formerly the dean of students at Southern Virginia University, where he served as a member of Virginia's Coalition on Alcohol Abuse. He is currently self-employed as a consultant and a professional writer and speaker, and is a member of the executive council of an adolescent treatment center in St. George, Utah. He is also currently contracted to provide training and lectures on adolescent addiction treatment for Hazelden Foundation.

Biddulph is a retired major in the U.S. Marine Corps and a decorated veteran of the Vietnam War, whose decorations include the Silver Star, the Purple Heart, the Meritorious Service Medal, and the Naval Achievement Medal. He is married to Elaine Robinson, and they are the parents of six children and twelve grandchildren. He and his wife currently reside in Provo, Utah.